A NEW SYSTEM OF EDUCATION

by

B. Everard Blanchard

An ETC Publication

1975

016015

C‖P

Library of Congress Cataloging in Publication Data

Blanchard, Birdsall Everard,   1909-
  A new system of education

  Bibliography: p.
  Includes index.
  1. Articulation (Education) 2. Education — United States
—1965-   II. Title.

LB2350.B54   371.2'18'0973   74-23970

ISBN 0-88280-012-4

Copyright © 1975 by ETC PUBLICATIONS
18512 Pierce Terrace
Homewood, Illinois 60430

Table of Contents

LIST OF CHARTS

LIST OF FIGURES

LIST OF TABLES

Page

This book is dedicated to
Ann, David, Sharon, and Kevin.

Preface

For some thirty years, the author has been experimenting with the organization, administration and supervisory functions of public schools and institutions of higher education.

The basic purpose of this book is to provide an overview of characteristic features of the American educational system together with a preview of the forces that necessitate change of structure.

Several challenges which face this country may be ennumerated as follows:

1. The increasing uncertainty of events plus the everpresent danger in our international relations which is attempting to strive toward a durable peace is the climate in which our present and future will be lodging. Peace is important today, because the ONLY alternative is destruction, or war.

2. People of different races, creeds, nationalities and places of residence must learn to live in harmony and with a mutual respect toward one another. In this area, the United States *must* set the pace if we are to gain the admiration, support and assistance we so need to continue our democratic way of life.

3. Discovering ways and means to use atomic energy for the benefit of all mankind. This necessarily will involve plans, policies, analysis, decision-making and the interpretative involvement of ALL people.

4. Computerization and automation may tend to foster an industrial revolution where technical competence may be replaced by machines. It will behoove people to acquire a mastery of high-level skills in order to be associated with the employed.

5. If machines replace man, increased production may decrease the job opportunities. What will the increased leisure be used for? As more emphasis may be upon the professional worker, he will have greater responsibilities and less leisure. What factors may affect these professionals?

6. On every hand, the values of society are changing. A re-commitment to values which will make life more important, seeing life as an adventure, a sense of dedication and loyalty needs to be stimulated by expert educational leadership. We need educational statesmen!

7. The mass organization of society is threatening the existence of the individual. To have to conform to mass ideas may steer one to rigidity and subject the individual to less mobility in creative thinking. Individual initiative may be stifled and personal development may be curtailed.

There are few educational issues which have given rise to less controversy in professional circles than that of articulation. However, the absence of controversy is not necessarily a good sign; it may simply reflect indifference and lack of information. It is quite possible that if several thousand educators were polled to name the major educational problems of our day, the mere mention of articulation would be rare indeed.

Since apathy and ignorance are the biggest obstacles to progress in utilizing articulation criteria more efficiently, it is only natural that some reliable data be presented to alert, not only the professional, but the layman as well. Thus the technical jargon commonly related to the vocabulary of the educator has been eliminated.

This compilation mirrors that effort to acquaint the general public as well as the professional educator with the facts as they exist and by the implementation of these facts in restructuring the American educational system.

The author wishes to acknowledge the assistance of some several thousand or more of public and private school teachers and administrators, college and university faculty and undergraduate and graduate students who volunteered as a participant. Without the cooperation of these fine people, this volume could not have been completed.

Finally, I desire to thank my wife, Ann, for her sincere encouragement which prodded me to complete this manuscript. The members of my family may now return to their normal pattern of living.

Villa Park, Illinois   B. Everard Blanchard

Foreword

As the old saying goes . . . if you don't know where you're going any road will take you there!

Dr. B. Everard Blanchard, through his national and regional surveys, knows where we are in the field of education . . . and he is zeroing in on where we should be going.

Dr. Blanchard considers the Carnegie Report on Education and also offers creative and innovative ideas and proposals of his own. This book can save the public not just millions, but billions of dollars in educational costs.

State Departments of Education and State Legislators should find this volume a vitally stimulating book with ideas deserving of experimental implementation. Dr. Blanchard proposes an entirely new elementary, secondary and higher education structure which may begin at the age of two, or three and extending through seventeen or eighteen . . . with earned bachelor's, or master's degrees. The multi-purpose proposed college would provide all American citizens with two years of FREE college level training. Prospective teachers would acquire twice as much training in professional and specialized work than is currently provided.

Undergraduate and graduate students will find this a meaningful, exciting and invigorating book which emphasizes the increased educational maturity of students at all levels. This increased maturity, Blanchard says, makes it possible and practical to reduce drastically the customary lock step of 8 and 4 years of formal education.

For anyone seriously interested in education . . . this book is the new cornerstone!

Dr. John E. Burns
Associate Professor of Management
De Paul University

CHAPTER 1
The Dilemma in Education

THE AMERICAN educational system is marked by great diversity and even by many contradictions. Someone has stated that the United States has no educational system and that within the parameters of the country can be found almost any practice the enquirer may seek.

Our midcentury prophets, from Walter Lippman and James B. Reston to the staff writers of *Newsweek,* have been telling us again and again that our colleges and universities are not placing the emphasis on "learning to learn." Thus, in 1940 in the Phi Beta Kappa lecture at the University of Pennsylvania, Lippman said: "Those who are responsible for modern education — for its controlling philosophy — are answerable for the results. They have determined the formation of the mind and education of modern men. As the tragic events unfold, they cannot evade their responsibility by talking about the crimes and follies of politicians, business men, labor leaders, lawyers, editors and generals — prevailing education is destined if it continues, to destroy Western Civilization, and is in fact destroying it."[1]

Despite all of the shared experiences and endless research, we continue to operate our educational systems without commonly accepted agreements about what the process of teaching should entail or what skills and knowledges are essential to teaching.[2]

If one wishes to know how other educators are solving the problems of the school; how curriculum practices may be affecting the learner; how teachers may be providing for individual differences; how guidance and counseling programs are being improved, etc., it appears logical that evidence substantiating such facts might be of some value.

Professional education stands at an historical juncture. Blind faith in education no longer is evidenced. Other professions, notably the medical, legal, and scientific — have evidenced substantial public reexamination. The question now is whether educators can continue to wander through the professional proving grounds without becoming equally as scarred as other professions. The danger of becoming an outdated and historical throwback is apparent. Massive loss of public confidence well might herald the erosion of professional integrity in education. Professional narrowness and philosophical inexactness only will encourage the arthritic and mortification process that has beset education. Viability in the future will depend upon the professional decisions that educators make.[3]

Standards in Education

There has been much talk about standards and about raising standards in American schools and colleges. Much less attention has been given to the problem of *what* these standards are. Louis Benezet asks whether excellence is necessarily manifested in "a high College Board aptitude score, a pattern of so many courses in prescribed subjects, an experience in a private school, and admission by one of some twenty-five 'prestige' colleges? ... If that impression is making headway — and I believe it is — then we have a long way to go in search for . . . Excellence . . . "[4]

There are some other questions that also need asking. How helpful or responsible is it

1. To endorse greater rigor in the selection of prospective teachers without suggesting what is meant by rigor or quality?
2. To endorse guidance without indicating what constitutes good counseling?
3. To recommend greater clarity and specificity with regard to institutional and program objectives without indicating what some of the specific objectives are?
4. To suggest that these objectives, still quite unidentified, constitute a desirable rationale for a school's admissions, curriculum, and evaluation practices?

5. To urge upon a college the desirability of determining what it considers to be the qualities desired in teachers and, hence, the qualifications of teachers without suggesting what at least some of these qualities and qualifications are?
6. To recommend an examination of the kinds and levels of tasks required of teachers without suggesting what they should be?
7. To continue to talk primarily about the supposed need for employing more teachers when the liklihood is that the problem cannot be solved without improving the ways in which teachers are used?
8. To urge that able students be selected without defining what is meant by an "able student" and without indicating how the selection will be made?

From the findings by the Newman Panel's *Report on Higher Education*, publicly endorsed by HEW, we may note the following points of view:

> . . . we have seen disturbing trends toward uniformity in our institutions, growing bureaucracy, overemphasized academic credentials, student and faculty isolation from the world — a growing rigidity and uniformity of structure that makes higher education reflect less and less the interests of society . . .

> The modern academic university has, like a magnet, drawn all institutions toward its organizational form, until the same teaching method, the same organization by disciplines, and the same professional academic training for faculty are nearly universal.

> While the population seeking higher education is becoming ever more diverse — in class and social background, age, academic experience, and ability — our colleges and universities . . . assume . . . only one mode of teaching and learning — the academic mode.

> Faculties . . . view themselves as independent professionals responsible to their guilds rather than to the institutions which pay their salaries.

> This organization of college curricula into the mold of the academic specialities has been accompanied by a strong

faculty bias towards the acquisition of theoretical knowledge. Numbers of students are refusing to submit to
answers prepackaged . . . by one of the conventional
disciplines.

We believe our colleges and universities must be less
concerned with academic prestige and more concerned
with becoming centers of effective learning.

From a speech by Dr. Fritz Machlup, Princeton economics
professor, printed in the February 28, 1974 issue of the *Washington
Post*, we may note:

Higher education is too high for the average intelligence,
much too high for the average interest, and vastly too high
for the average patience and perseverance of the people,
here and anywhere. Attempts to expose from 30 to 50 percent of the people to higher education are completely
useless.

Longer education (beyond high school) has become the
marching order of our society, but since it cannot aspire
to provide higher learning, longer education can only be
thinner or broader.

There is nothing new about the fact that colleges and
universities include elementary and secondary education
in their programs; the question is merely whether the
share of higher education has been diminishing.

I define higher education as the level of scholarly
teaching, learning, and researching that is accessible to
only a small fraction of people.

I firmly believe that higher education should be open to
all who want it and can take it . . . But we cannot change
the fact that perhaps 80 percent of the people find it 'not
relevant' to their interests and capacities.

Broader, continuing education also should be open to all
who want it, and many more will be qualified for it.

What I deplore is that virtually all colleges and universities are reducing academic requirements and the level of

their offerings in the name of social justice and equality of opportunity — that is, in order to accommodate more of those who are not prepared to take higher education.

In a number of speeches President Edward H. Levi of the University of Chicago has proposed major reforms in higher education. Because "the length of time required for training in some of the professions is a national disgrace" and because "in the last analysis it is only self-education which counts," he proposed a number of reforms:[5]

1. A degree for general education after two years of college work;
2. Hence, earlier admission into graduate and professional schools;
3. Reduction of time spent in graduate and professional work;
4. A system of national examinations for individuals who might not be connected with any formal institution;
5. Development of different kinds of institutions with more flexible programs.

"A more open system has risks," President Levi stated, "but it could reassemble to greater advantage the strength which is there."

A study group of the *American Academy of Arts and Sciences* has urged that college students be allowed to interrupt their studies for long periods and that adults, with or without degrees, be given much easier access to undergraduate and graduate programs. "There is no rhythm or pattern of intellectual curiosity or social maturity common to all," the study group stated.

"What a young person may not wish to do at 18 or 22 he or she may be very interested in pursuing at 30 or 40."

The study group called for an end to the "near monopoly" of the Ph.D. degree as a college teaching license, suggesting instead that an "honors" bachelor's degree might be substituted. It said that graduate programs should be shortened and that graduate students heading for teaching should have supervised apprenticeships.[6]

The former U.S. Commissioner of Education S.P. Marland, Jr., appearing before the Convention of the *National Association of Secondary-School Principals* in Houston, had this to say: Get rid of the "academic snobbery" that created and now perpetuates the "false dichotomy between things academic and things vocational." He decried general education as "neither fish nor fowl, neither truly vocational nor truly academic," and he suggested that we get rid of it, too.[7]

The Commissioner advised that, until a new system for contemporary career development can be recommended, an interim strategy of four major actions be developed and employed:[8]

1. To improve the vocational program of the U.S. Office of Education in order to give the States new leadership and technical support in shaping their programs to satisfy existing and future national occupational needs.
2. To provide high school graduates with more flexible options in continuing their education or entering the work force.
3. To bring business, industry, and labor in closer collaboration with the schools.
4. To build a new leadership and commitment to the concept of a career education system.

Relative to the elimination of *general education* as advocated by the former U.S. Commissioner of Education S. P. Marland, Jr., Garwood states:[9]

> Washington is full of men and women who can master a part of the problems and look after the means, but not of men who can encompass the larger question of the ends or purposes of our activities. In short, our technical education, aiming at efficiency and practical results for limited ends, seems to be more successful than our liberal education which is supposed to inform and train our minds in everything from logical analysis to aesthetic appreciation and also to teach us to integrate the facts that are relevant to our lives.

Radical changes to create a "comprehensive plan of teacher education for the United States" have been proposed in a report on *Teachers for the Real World*, published by the American Association of Colleges for Teacher Education. "Education is beyond repair! What is needed is radical reform. This reform is to include the nature of the schooling process, the systems which control educational policy, and the institutions which prepare persons to be teachers," the report suggested.[10]

Realities in Education

Let us review for the moment, some of the facts as may exist in our educational system. *First*, there appears to be little relationship between the earmarks of success in school and subsequent demonstration of those virtues inherent in many statements of educational aims. Marks in school subjects are virtually useless as predictors of creativity, inventiveness, leadership, good citizenship, personal and social maturity, family happiness, and honest workmanship.[11] Either we are not rewarding or we are not providing adequately (or both) for development of qualities so frequently set forth in statements of educational goals.

Second, there is an unwillingness or an inability (or both) to state — at any level of responsibility or authority — what purposes are to be served by education, schools, or specific programs of instruction. States are confused as to their freedom and responsibilities in this regard and do not define adequately the role of their departments of education, as any cursory examination of state courses of study quickly reveals. Local school boards are assiduous in their avoidance of the issues involved, failing to take advantage of American pluralism. When the prospect of determining educational goals at the federal level of responsibility looms, we cry local autonomy — failing to realize that we have a vacuum here into which spill the wares of remote curriculum builders. There should be small wonder that many educators have little stomach for the determination of educational objectives.[12]

Third, the common expectation and demonstrated function of our schools are to cover tasks and materials that have been predetermined for specific grades and periods of time.[13] This condition does not have a sound pedagogical base. It denies our growing awareness of individual differences in learning and of the probability that *what children learn* has more to do with whether or not they are *exposed* to it, than to our genius in the grade placement of children and content.

Fourth, a substantial portion of the curriculum has not been justified on criteria other than habit or tradition. This is particularly true in the social studies where too many insignificant historical events are learned by rote, where homogenized community studies predominate in the lower years, and where a "mankind" approach is largely lacking.

Fifth, the separate-subject pattern of curriculum organization that has predominated during the past decade of curriculum reform has placed profound problems of choice upon local school districts.[14] There simply cannot be thirty or more academic disciplines in the kindergarten. Further, the strenghtening of subjects already in the curriculum through massive federal grants (largely from the National Science Foundation) has not enhanced the status of relatively new but nonetheless important disciplines.

Sixth, the much-heralded pedagogical revolution is still largely in the cumulo-nimbus clouds of educational reform that roll back and forth across this vast and varied land. These clouds have not yet enveloped the millions of teachers who make up the working force of our elementary and secondary schools to anything like the high degree claimed by many innovators and popular magazines. To be specific, teaching is still largely a "telling" procedure, with exchanges being primarily between teacher and child rather than among groups of children. The processes of "discovery" and "inquiry" — so lauded by curriculum reformers — seem not to be well understood and tend to be used mechanically, if at all. The textbook dominates instruction. Films when used, more often than not are supplementary and are not woven into the fabric of the program. It is difficult to detect in the classroom common use of such psychologocal concepts as goal setting, motivation, positive reinforcement, evaluative checking, and so on. The class usually is instructed as a whole, except for the common practice of achievement grouping for reading in the primary grades and of some grouping in mathematics. The technological revolution has scarcely ruffled most classrooms; the computer is used for routine data processing in large school systems and for instructional purposes in only a handful of experimental laboratories.[15]

Seventh, innovations which, in concept, are designed to unshackle the restrictive, monolithic structure of schools appear often to be tacked on. Nongrading is supposed to raise the ceilings and lower the floors of expectancy for the class group, reduce the importance of age as a factor in determining the student's program, encourage greater flexibility in grouping practices, and so on. But a study of the supposed nongraded elementary schools in the United States found little movement in these directions.[16] Nongrading, team teaching, and other innovations of potential power are far from simple in concept and implementation. Are we expecting too much in attempting them apart from simulation, demonstration, and the kind of in-service teacher education that has characterized recent curriculum reform?

Eighth, there is precious little experimentation with the school as an educational instrument. A recent poll suggests that the lay public is at least as ready for change as the educators.[17] But there always seems to be enough resistance on the part of vocal parents and entrenched professionals to cause undue caution on the part of administrators. At least one highly visible school principal is convinced that his administrative colleagues are not now giving the leadership that we need — and that is possible, even within the existing structure of American education.[18] Do we need schools whose very reason for existence is experimentation and innovation?

Ninth, teacher education (the whole of the program — not just to the education courses), which should be the fountainhead, too often is a drainage ditch. There is no point in entering now into the problems and issues of what James B. Conant has called "that can of worms." They have been well documented elsewhere.[19] It seems apparent that *nothing short of a complete overhaul will bring to our teacher education programs, both preservice and inservice, the vitality they must have if teachers are to effect the rapid educational evolution we want.*

Tenth, there is an assumption abroad in the land that the task before us now is to implement a host of educational innovations which already have been amply demonstrated and proved worthy. This is, to a degree, accompanied by the assumption that federal intervention has created a self-renewing mechanism of supplementary and regional laboratories that will provide the new forms and substances we need for 1980 and beyond. These are uneasy assumptions.

Regarding the first assumption, we have had but a handful of potent, imaginative, educational innovations during the past decade or so. Further, we have had very little detailed development and demonstration of these and very little interpretation or testing of the assumptions underlying them. Widespread dissemination of what we rather dimly perceive will occupy much time and energy, but whether it will profoundly change or improve education is questionable.

Regarding the second assumption, we need, in addition to our action-oriented enterprises, a much greater commitment to protected, funded, and superbly staffed, long-term inquiry of a sort that neither the federal government nor the private foundation is now providing.[20]

[1]John D. Garwood, "The Wrong Premise in General Education," *Intellect*, 102 (October 1973), 43.

[2]Castelle Gentry and Charles Johnson, *A Practical Management System For Performance-Based Teacher Education*, American Association of Colleges for Teacher Education (February 1974), 1.

[3]J. Merrell Hansen, "The Handwriting on the Professional Wall," *Intellect*, 102 (October 1973), 23.

[4]Winslow R. Hatch, Director, Clearinghouse of Studies on Higher Education, Division of Higher Education. New Dimensions in Higher Education, Number 12, OE-53019. *What Standards Do We Raise?* U.S. Department of Health, Education, and Welfare, Washington, D.C., 1964, p. 4.

[5]*The University of Chicago Magazine*, Quadrangle News, Vol. LXIII, No. 3, January-February 1971, p. 28.

[6]*Today's Education*, The Journal of the National Education Association, Vol. 60, No. 4, April 1971, p. 4.

[7]*American Education*, U.S. Department of Health, Education, and Welfare, Office of Education, Washington, D.C., March 1971. From *The Editor* page.

[8]*Ibid.*, *The Editor* page.

[9]*Op Cit.*, p. 43.

[10]*Phi Delta Kappan*, Vol. L, No. 9, May 1969, p. 546.

[11]C. Robert Pace, "Perspectives on the Student and His College," *The College and the Student*, edited by Lawrence Dennis and Joseph Kaufman (Washington, D.C.: American Council on Education, 1966), p. 76-100.

[12]Margaret P. Ammons, "Educational Objectives: The Relation between the Process Used in Their Development and Their Quality," (Unpublished doctoral dissertation, University of Chicago, 1961).

[13]This and several subsequent observations are based on data from a report by John I. Goodlad and Associates, *A Study of Childhood Schooling*. Study conducted under a grant from the Fund for the Advancement of Education of the Ford Foundation.

[14]See John I. Goodlad and Associates, *The Changing School Curriculum* (New York: Fund for the Advancement of Education, 1966).

[15]See John I. Goodlad, John F. O'Toole, Jr., and Louise L. Tyler, *Computers and Information Systems in Education* (New York: Harcourt, Brace, and World, Inc., 1966).

[16]Delgado-Marcano, Maria T., "The Operation of Curriculum and Instruction in Twenty Nongraded Elementary Schools" (Submitted in partial fulfillment of the requirements for the Doctor of Education degree in the School of Education, Indiana University, September, 1965).

[17]"Parents Are Ready; a Report of a Gallup Poll Measuring Public Reactions," *The Instructor*, 76 (October, 1966), pp. 149, 154.

[18]Brown, B. Frank, *The Nongraded High School* (Englewood Cliffs, N.J.: Prentice-Hall, Inc., 1963).

[19]See, for example, James B. Conant, *The Education of American Teachers* (New York: McGraw-Hill, 1963).

[20]*Implications for Education of Prospective Changes in Society: Designing Education for the Future: An Eight-State Project.* Edited by Edgar L. Morphet and Charles O. Ryan. Financed by funds provided under the Elementary and Secondary Education Acts of 1965 (Public Law 89-10, Title V, Sec. 505) and the Sponsoring States. Bradford-Ribinson Ptg., Company, Denver, Colorado, January, 1967, pp. 51-52.

CHAPTER 2
U.S. Citizens: Educational
Attainment and Job Profile

WITH A SYSTEM of education which is supposed to be superior to all other systems in the world, some 55 percent of our people have less than four years of high school education. Unless something is done immediately to lower this percentage who lack an adequate high school education, our nation is heading toward a catastrophic future.

Our entire educational system from the preschool level through the graduate school needs to be "restructured" as this volume will suggest throughout its following pages. Merely changing subject matter, methodology, content, evaluation techniques, etc., will have no appreciable effect on upgrading the education of American citizenry.

The North Central Association in the *Annual Report for 1971* makes a number of statements in the mood of the following:

> . . . higher education is breaking out of its structural bonds. Bold new ventures which do more than modify old structures are upon us — ventures truly innovative in their rejection of old patterns. The Commission believes that a newer and broader sense of education is emerging and that new structures, new modes of teaching and learning, and other types of arrangements will be initiated, developing within or alongside the more traditional educational institution. The Commission has underway plans for revising its procedures and evaluative techniques in a fashion consistent with the new developments . . .[1]

A major lesson which seems to emanate from these projections is the need for greater flexibility in training teachers and in utilizing educational resources. Continued swings of considerable magnitude in the size of the preschool educational pattern, the reorganization of the elementary, secondary, and college structure are indeed in prospect the remainder of this century.

One way to view the *necessity* of "restructuring" our American educational ladder is to review the educational attainment of our major ethnic groups. For example, Figure 1 indicates persons 25 years old and over, the years of schooling completed by percent, those individuals with four years of high school or more, and those individuals with some college, or four or more years. The results should be of *immediate concern* to those administrators responsible for directing the educational programs in our country. However, these figures may have as much effect upon the bureaucracy of the Educational Establishment as it would be to measure a brick with a micrometer!

Figure 2-1 tends to show that of the several ethnic groups reviewed, the *Puerto Ricans* lead the parade in this country with an

FIGURE 2-1
Educational Attainment of Major Ethnic Origin Groups[2]

	Total population	Number	Persons 25 years old and over			
			Years of school completed by percent			
			Less than 4 yrs. H.S.	4 years of H.S. or more		
					Some college	
				Total	Total	4 or more
Total	198,214,000	106,284,000	44.8	55.2	21.3	11.0
English	19,060,000	11,999,000	39.8	60.2	26.6	14.4
German	19,961,000	12,825,000	42.4	57.6	20.4	10.5
Irish	13,282,000	8,630,000	44.7	55.3	20.0	10.2
Italian	7,239,000	4,683,000	54.3	45.7	13.7	7.0
Polish	4,021,000	2,769,000	49.1	50.9	15.8	8.8
Russian . . .	2,152,000	1,584,000	30.9	69.1	35.4	22.9
Spanish:						
Central or						
So. America	556,000	273,000	46.2	53.8	24.5	11.2
Cuban . . .	565,000	320,000	47.8	52.2	24.7	12.7
Mexican .	5,073,000	1,909,000	75.6	24.4	6.4	1.6
Puerto Rican	1,454,000	549,000	77.8	22.0	5.6	2.4
Other Spanish	1,582,000	766,000	47.7	52.2	19.8	8.7
All other	105,633,000	49,286,000	43.2	56.8	22.9	11.6
Not reported[3]	17,635,000	10,692,000	50.1	50.0	16.6	8.4

estimated 77.8 percent having less than four years of secondary education; the *Mexicans* follow with 75.6 percent; next we find the *Italians* with 54.3 percent; the *Polish* with 49.1 percent; the *Cubans* with 47.8 percent and *Other Spanish*, 47.7 percent.

Of the six groups reviewed, approximately 6,191,176 or 56 percent of the total population of 10,966,000 had less than four years of high school training.

Some 22.0 percent of the *Puerto Ricans* have had four years of high school or more; *Mexicans* have 24.4 percent; *Italians* have 45.7 percent; *Polish* have 50.9 percent; *Cubans* and *Other Spanish* have 52.2 percent.

Relative to some college training, the *Puerto Ricans* have the least, 5.6 percent; the *Mexicans*, 6.4 percent; the *Italians*, 13.7 percent; the *Polish*, 15.8 percent; *Other Spanish*, 19.8 percent and the *Irish*, 20.0 percent.

Relative to four years or more of college education, we find *Mexicans* behind all other ethnic groups with only 1.6 percent of their population attaining such training. Next, we find the *Puerto Ricans* at 2.4 percent; *Italians* at 7.0 percent; *Other Spanish* at 8.7 percent; *Polish* at 8.8 percent and the *Irish* at 10.2 percent.

Since learning and earning are closely associated with one another, we might state that the ethnic groups in this country today are living in economic strait-jackets.

Of all employed men age 25 to 64 without high school diplomas, 33 percent had 1971 incomes of less than $6,000. Only 13 percent of this age group with diplomas had incomes below $6,000. Conversely, only 6 percent of the men without high school diplomas had incomes over $15,000 while 22 percent of men with diplomas and 43 percent of those with college degrees had incomes above $15,000.[4]

Directly connected with these income figures is the type of work done by those who complete high school compared to those who do not. In 1972, only 9 percent of those without diplomas were working in professional, technical or managerial positions. But of those with a diploma, 21 percent held positions of this sort, while of those with a college degree an astonishing 80 percent were in these top white collar jobs.[5]

Professor John D. Garwood has stated: Enough new information to fill a 24-volume set of *Encyclopedia Britannica* is added to the world's libraries every 40 minutes. The U.S. Government alone generates 100,000 reports and publishes 450,000 articles, books, and papers annually. On a world basis, 60,000,000 pages of scientific and technical literature are published per annum.[6] Such an explosion of knowledge requires a highly literate population to make effective use of it.

Although no one can accurately forecast the future, we may project the attitude, that if the disparities in the education of our major ethnic groups continue along traditional paths with no effort made by the Educational Establishment to provide these individuals with adequate personal, educational and vocational career guidance and competencies — the future will see public relief rolls, unemployment, crime, civil disorders and the like increase as has never been witnessed by this nation. This type of internal insecurity may also endanger our international relationships with other countries with whom we have been striving to achieve a durable peace. Peace is important, because the only alternative is destruction, or war. It is impossible to provide a world leadership of a statesmanlike character when we cannot settle our own problems in an amenable manner.

Industry Profile

Perhaps, if we but review the facts as related to industrial composition and how it affects employment, educators if susceptible, might be able to revitalize the services rendered American youth in public and private schools throughout the country.

Most of the Nation's workers are in service-producing industries, which include activities such as education, health care, trade, repair and maintenance, government, transportation, banking, and insurance. These industries employed 80 percent of all college graduates in the labor force in 1970.[7] With a range from only 1.6 to 22.9 percent of our major ethnic groups having four or more years of college training, the future prospects relative to securing decent jobs appears dismal for Mexicans, Puerto Ricans, Italians, Spanish, and Polish people.

The production of goods — farming, building, extracting minerals, and manufacturing — has required less than half of the country's work force since the late 1940's. Approximately 20 percent of the Nation's college graduates were employed in these industries in 1970. Chart 2-1 illustrates the Nation's industrial composition:

CHART 2-1 — Where people work[8]
Employment, 1970 (millions of workers)*

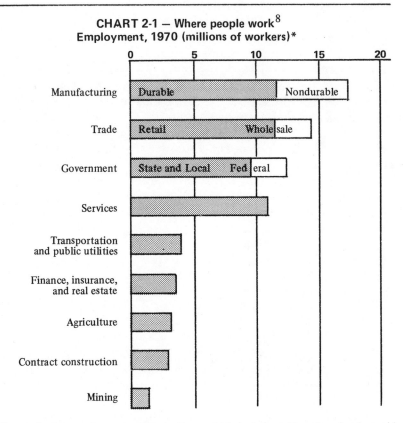

*Wage and salary workers, except agriculture, which includes self-employed and unpaid family workers.
Source: Bureau of Labor Statistics.

In general, job growth through the 1970's is expected to continue to be faster in the service-producing industries than in the goods-producing industries. However, among industry divisions in both the goods and service-producing sectors, the growth pattern will vary.[9] (See Chart 2-2).

Service-Producing Industries

In 1970, 47.3 million workers were on the payrolls of service-producing industries — government; wholesale and retail trade; services such as education, health, and recreation; transportation,

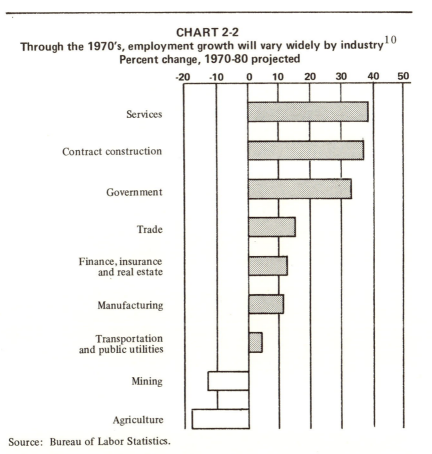

CHART 2-2
Through the 1970's, employment growth will vary widely by industry[10]
Percent change, 1970-80 projected

Source: Bureau of Labor Statistics.

communication, and other utilities; and finance, insurance, and real estate. This was 13.5 million more than the number employed in 1960. The major factors underlying this rapid growth were (1) population growth; (2) increasing urbanization; and (3) rising incomes and living standards and the accompanying demand for improved health, education, recreation and security service.[11] (See Chart 2-3).

Of the 47.3 million workers in service-producing industries in 1970, 16 percent or 7.7 million were college graduates. (A "college graduate" refers to a person who has completed 4 or more years of college work, whether or not he or she holds a college degree.) The expected rapid growth in the service-producing industries, where employment is projected to increase by 26 percent, reaching 59.5

CHART 2-3
Industries providing services offer more jobs than those providing goods[12]
Workers (in millions)*

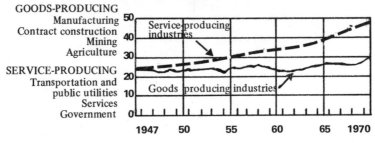

GOODS-PRODUCING
Manufacturing
Contract construction
Mining
Agriculture

SERVICE-PRODUCING
Transportation and
public utilities
Services
Government

*Wage and salary workers, except agriculture, which includes self-employed and unpaid family workers.

Source: Bureau of Labor Statistics.

million by 1980, should result in a rapid rise in demand for college educated workers in these industries.[13]

During 1970, employment was 14.9 million, 31 percent above the 1960 level in *Trade* because wholesale and retail outlets have increased in large and small cities to meet the needs of an increasingly urban society. Approximately 910,000 or 6 percent of the workers in trade were college graduates.

Government employment increased by an estimated 50 percent from 8.4 million in 1960 to 12.6 million in 1970. Growth has been mostly at the State and local levels which, combined, increased by almost two-thirds. It appears that government employment is a major area for college educated workers. Almost 30 percent of Government employees, 3.7 million in 1970, were college graduates. By 1980, employment may be as much as 33 percent higher than in 1970.[14]

Service and miscellaneous industries employment has increased rapidly in recent years due to the growing demand for maintenance and repair, advertising, domestic, and health care services. From 1960 to 1970, total employment in this industry division rose by about two-fifths from about 8 million to 11.6 million. In 1970, approximately 2.2 million (19 percent) were college graduates.

Transportation and public utilities employment in 1970, at 4.5 million, was only slightly more than one-tenth higher than in 1960. In 1970, approximately 5 percent, or 234,000 of these workers, were college graduates. Overall employment in these industries is expected to increase to more than 4.7 million in 1980, 5 percent above the 1970 level.

Finance, insurance, and real estate, which has the smallest number of workers of the service-producing industries, grew 38 percent since 1960, from 2.7 million to 3.7 million in 1970. Sixteen percent of the workers, or almost 600,000 were college graduates. Employment grew especially rapidly in banking, credit agencies, security and commodity brokers, and dealer's exchanges.

Goods-Producing Industries

Almost two million workers in goods-producing industries were college graduates in 1970. Employment in these areas is expected to increase to 12 percent above the 1970 level by 1980.

For example, *manufacturing,* the largest division within the goods-producing sector, employed 19.4 million workers in 1970, an increase of 16 percent over 1960. An estimated 8 percent of the workers, or 1.6 million, were college graduates. Manufacturing employment is expected to increase by 13 percent through the 1970's and reach 21.9 million in 1980.

Agriculture, which until the late 1800's employed more than half of all workers, employed only 5 percent, or 3.4 million, in 1970. Slightly more than 105,000, about 3 percent of the total, were college graduates.

Contract construction employment, at more than 3.3 million in 1970, increased more than one-sixth from 1960. In 1970, approximately 4 percent of the workers, or 125,000 were college graduates.

Mining employment, at about 620,000 in 1970, declined by nearly 13 percent from 1960, primarily because of laborsaving technological changes and a shift to sources of power other than coal. The mining industry, however, has the highest proportion of college educated workers among the goods-producing industries. In 1970, 12 percent of the employees, almost 75,000 were college graduates. Total employment in mining is expected to decline to about 550,000 by 1980, 12 percent below the 1970 level.

Occupational Profile

In 1965, for the first time in the Nation's history, white-collar workers — professional, managerial, clerical, and sales — outnumbered blue-collar workers — craftsmen, operatives, and laborers.

Total employment is expected to increase 21 percent between 1970 and 1980. Employment of white-collar workers is expected to increase by 27 percent, while blue-collar employment is expected to increase by only 12 percent. By 1980, white-collar workers will account for more than one-half of all employed workers, compared with 48 percent in 1970.

White-collar employment opportunities and the rapid growth in professional occupations is steadily increasing the proportion of college graduates in the labor force. For example, in 1962, 11.5 percent of all workers were college graduates. By 1970, approximately 13 percent or 10 million of the 78.6 million workers in the labor force were college graduates. By 1980, 16.8 percent — over 15.9 million workers — are expected to be college graduates. Among reasons for the growth in the employment of college graduates are: (1) Employers are seeking people who have higher levels of education because jobs are more complex and require greater skill; (2) employment in those occupations requiring the most education, for example, professional occupations, will show the fastest growth through the 1970's; and (3) through the 1970's the number of young workers will increase and these workers will have more education on the average than did new entrants to the labor force in previous years.[15]

The changes that are expected to occur among the occupational groups through the 1970's are described as follows:

White-collar workers — professional and technical, managers, clerical and sales workers — numbered about 38 million in 1970. Approximately 25 percent or 9.5 million were college graduates. In 1980, 32 percent or 15.3 million of the projected 48.3 million white-collar workers are expected to be college graduates. (See Chart 2-4).

Professional and technical workers, the third largest occupational group in 1970, with more than 11.1 million workers, include such highly trained personnel as doctors, teachers, engineers, dentists, accountants, and clergymen.

It is believed that professional occupations will be the fastest growing occupational group to 1980. Increased emphasis on socioeconomic progress, urban renewal, transportation, harnessing the ocean, and on the environment will account for an expected 40 percent increase among professional, technical, and kindred workers.

CHART 2-4

College graduates are primarily in white-collar occupations[16]
Workers, 1970 (in millions)

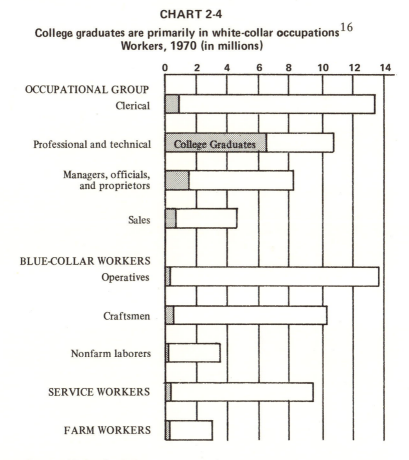

Source: Bureau of Labor Statistics.

Almost 60 percent (6.7 million) of all professional and technical workers were college graduates in 1970. If present trends continue, more than two-thirds, 10.5 million, of the projected 15.5 million workers in the group will be college graduates in 1980.

Managers, officials, and proprietors totaled 8.3 million in 1970 and are expected to grow at a somewhat slower rate (15 percent) than the average for all groups. The employment of college graduates is expected to increase from 1.7 million to about 2.9 million.

Clerical workers, numbering 13.7 million in 1970, include workers who operate computers and office machines, keep records, take dictation, and type. Employment of such personnel is expected to increase by more than one-fourth between 1970 and 1980. Roughly 5 percent or 650,000 clerical and related workers were college graduates in 1970. This proportion is depicted as remaining stable through the 1970's.

Salesworkers, 4.9 million in 1970, are found in retail stores, wholesale firms, insurance companies, real estate agencies, manufacturing firms, and firms offering goods door to door. Between 1970 and 1980, employment of sales-workers is expected to increase by almost one-fourth to 6 million. In 1970, 570,000 persons, 12 percent of the total in sales occupations, were college graduates. By 1980, the proportion is projected to reach 17 percent and number approximately 1 million.

The Blue-collar occupational groups — craftsmen, operatives, and laborers — employ small percentages of college and university graduates. For example, in 1970, only about 1 percent of the 27.8 million blue-collar workers were college graduates.

Service workers, including men and women who provide protective services, assist professional nurses in hospitals, give haircuts and beauty treatments, serve food, and clean and care for homes, totaled 9.7 million in 1970. Employments requirements for this diverse group will increase about 35 percent between 1970 and 1980. In 1970, only about 1 percent of service workers, or 130,000 were college graduates, and about the same proportion is expected by 1980.

Farm workers, including farmers, farm managers, laborers, and foremen numbered about 3.1 million in 1970. Employment requirements for farm workers are expected to decline to 2.6 million in 1980. Just over 1 percent of all farm workers were college graduates in 1970; this may increase to 2 percent by 1980, if past trends continue.

The brief review of business and industrial requirements reported thus far has emphasized the increasing demands for college graduates. Sad to say, America's institutions of higher education, as well as business and industry, are ACADEMIC CREDENTIAL conscious. A degree, per se, is no guarantee of competence — never has been and likely never will be.

Unless America's plans of educating all American youth is changed drastically within the next ten-year period, the varied ethnic groups discussed earlier with less than four years of secondary education will undergo the stress of a pregnant mother — "labor pains."

In many areas of the country today, school authorities are now encouraging high schoolers to enter vocational and industrial training. Some are beginning programs at the kindergarten level to convince pupils and their parents that trades and technical skills are valuable and worth considering.

Why the sudden switch away from stressing a four-year college education? The change seems to stem from increasing demand for skilled workers and the current unemployment of many college graduates — especially those with *liberal arts degrees*.[17]

With a civilian labor force during 1973, the first half average, persons 16 years of age and over, out of a total 87,529,000, an estimated 83,053,000 were employed and approximately 4,476,000 unemployed. If the United States continues its traditional educational pattern, we may expect the unemployment trend to increase, from approximately 5 percent to roughly 10 percent within the next two decades.

A New Route

We need a revised commitment to American education. A commitment which will provide every American citizen from 2 or 3 years of age through 17 or 18, a free public education which will provide numerous options and which will consume less time. Additionally, this new education will result in each American citizen achieving a rich and abundant source of ideas, and the opportunity to acquire a variety of marketable skills in at least TWO areas of competency. By so doing, we shall decrease unemployment to a negligible figure; we shall diminish the public welfare group in that everyone, physically and mentally capable can work (the word retirement will exist only in the dictionary); we shall thus enable the dignity and the individuality of man to emerge in a fashion never before realized by man.

The NEW ROUTE is not so much to impart knowledge to citizens, as to whet the appetite, exhibit methods, develop powers, strengthen judgment, and invigorate the intellectual, moral, social, emotional and spiritual forces. The NEW ROUTE will prepare individuals for the service to be achieved by society, through wise, thoughtful, and progressive guides in whatever zone of work or thought humans may be engaged.

1North Central Association of Colleges and Secondary Schools, *Annual Report 1971*: Commission on Institutions of Higher Education, Chicago, NCA, 1972, pp. 2-6.

2Source: November 1969 Current Population Survey of the Bureau of the Census.

3Includes persons who reported that they did not know their ethnic origin.

4"Learning and Earning," *The World Almanac and Book of Facts*, 1974, p. 315.

5*Ibid.*, p. 315.

6*Op. Cit.*, p. 43.

7U.S. Department of Labor, Bureau of Labor Statistics, *Occupational Outlook for College Graduates 1972-73 Edition*, Bulletin 1730 (Washington, D.C., 20212) p. 1.

8*Ibid.*, p. 2.

9*Ibid.*, p. 1.

10*Ibid.*, p. 2.

11*Ibid.*, p. 1.

12*Ibid.*, p. 3.

13*Ibid.*, pp. 1-2.

14*Ibid.*, p. 2.

15*Ibid.*, pp. 4-5.

16*Ibid.*, p. 5.

17Pamela Swift, "Keeping Up . . . With Youth — New Status," *Parade*, March 31, 1974, p. 26.

✿

CHAPTER 3
A National Survey:
Curriculum Articulation Between
the College of Liberal Arts
and the Secondary School[1]

THE USUAL procedure in writing a book is to develop a thesis, examine the evidence and present conclusions supported by the data. At this point then, let us review the evidence which tends to support the author's contention that a "restructuring" of education is absolutely necessary to meet the challenges of contemporary and the emerging society.

Introduction

The name by which an institution is known is not always a trustworthy index of the level at which it renders service. There are some colleges and universities which are nothing more than mediocre high schools. The charter granted an institution should not be taken at face value. Regional and/or state accreditation are not always credible.

If one is concerned with higher education in terms of objectives, a little probing indicates that the objectives of higher education do not differ significantly in many instances from those educational objectives utilized in secondary education. Or, one might be interested in defining higher education in terms of methods of instruction or methods of study, however, it may be noted that here again, higher education does not differ sharply in these respects from other levels of education.

In brief, higher education may be defined as that level of education which lies beyond the completion of high school. We are concerned basically with the liberal arts college; this is typically an institution offering the Bachelor's degree on the basis of a four-year program beyond the completion of high school. A few of the stronger liberal arts colleges also offer a fifth year of work leading to the Master's degree in some subject-matter fields.

Review of the Literature

We have been schooled on catalogue prose that describes a list of educational aims and then assures its clientele that these aims are regularly accomplished by the faculty, having first been laid down by the administration and approved by the board of trustees. Meanwhile, the supporting evidence of such accomplishment remains thin.[2]

Two important books published in the first part of 1968 — *The Higher Learning in America: A Reassessment*[3] by Paul Woodring, and *The Academic Revolution*[4] by Jencks and Riesman, make the point that whereas faculty devaluation of undergraduate teaching, particularly of courses in liberal education, has been a major factor in student disaffection, students tend to blame the administration and not the professors for their feelings of alienation.

Benezet believes[5] that chief among the things that have not changed in the American college are the methods of teaching liberal education. The testimony of Julian Ross speaks for the liberal arts colleges everywhere:

> Though the liberal arts curriculum has passed through a cycle of changes, such as the rise and decline of general education courses, it is now very similar to what it was in 1925. Both then and now it included requirements in foreign language, laboratory science, a series of distribution courses, and a thirty hour major.

The role of general education has experienced numerous interpretations. For example, Cowley (1960) cited the belief in some quarters that general education properly belongs in secondary schools. He cited the disinterest of a substantial portion of faculty members, the dominant status of the research function, and the present major system as tending to emphasize special rather than general education.[6]

De Vane (1964) noting the trends toward early and narrow specialization, as more students press toward graduate and professional schools, expressed concern that widespread advanced placement may sacrifice the cohesive effect of the common curriculum in the early years of college. However, to the extent that secondary schools relieve colleges of basic studies such as English composition, calculus, and foreign language, De Vane stated, advanced placement has merit.[7]

In a study restricted to catalogued documentation of 28 liberal arts colleges, Rudy (1960) found a trend in which general education was confined in varying degrees to the first two years, followed by specialized and even professional training. Reflecting this emphasis, faculties were organized on the basis of specialized department areas of scholarly and professional interest. In only a few nationally renowned liberal arts colleges and Catholic colleges was the trend less sweeping. St. John's College, Annapolis, Maryland, represents a case having little influence on the main line of development.[8]

McGrath (1961, 1963a) studied the curricula of 14 independent liberal arts colleges and related costs of instruction. He found that subject matter splintering and course proliferation produced not only a meager body of undergraduate common instruction but also many courses of a postgraduate character with few students and an overworked and underpaid faculty.[9,10]

Brinker (1960) studied courses taken by liberal arts students in four liberal arts colleges of the Southwest to validate the presumption that a well educated liberal arts graduate should have at least an acquaintance with humanities, social sciences, and natural science. The study found that humanities and science majors failed to obtain an elementary acquaintance with disciplines in other fields and that graduates of three of the colleges concentrated in their majors, sacrificing breadth for depth. There is some evidence that advisers were motivated to enhance the prestige of their own Departments rather than to see merit in other disciplines.[11]

The place and nature of general education remains unsettled and articulation with secondary schools is a renewed concern. Faculty responsibilities in curriculum planning and development do not appear to have reached any amicable agreement. The need for more constructive definitive research is a perennial one, especially in the area of curricula for higher education. It would seem that the increasing tempo of change should bring with it commensurate attention to experimentation and research as necessary to direct such change.

Evidence of faulty articulation in our educational system exists when there is overlapping of subject-matter content at various levels. One of the earliest studies which displays incoordination of this type is that of Osburn.[12] His investigation sought to determine the extent to which the subject-matter at one level of the educational system is the same as that at another level. His results show that 17 per cent of the course in high-school physics is repeated in college. One-fifth of the high-school English course is presented earlier in the elementary schools and one-tenth of it is presented over again in the college unit. Almost 20 per cent of the content of high-school history was found to have been taught in the elementary grades, and almost 23 per cent of it is taught again in college.

A candidate for the Bachelor's degree in college who has specialized in English will probably have studied Shakespeare's "Julius Caesar" some four times during his school program in the elementary grades, high school, and college. Examples of this type of overlapping can readily be multiplied.[13]

Purpose of Study

The basic purpose of this study was to determine the degree of articulation between high school and college level subject-matter. Precisely, the investigator wished to determine what the relative amount of overlapping or duplication there might be between the first two years of liberal arts college education and the last two years of the secondary school in the areas of English, science, social studies, and mathematics.

Sampling Population

An estimated 269 colleges and universities, or 60 per cent of those listed in the *Thirteenth Annual List*[14] (effective, September 1, 1966 to August 31, 1967) of the *National Council for Accreditation of*

Teacher Education (NCATE) comprised one of the samples used in the study.

Approximately 400 college faculty members representing these colleges and universities carefully reviewed high school courses in the areas of English, science, social studies, and mathematics.

Some 800 secondary schools selected at random from the roster of each of the six regional accreditation associations were invited to participate in this study. Of the 800, some 65 per cent, or 520 high schools representing some forty-one states became the second sample utilized in this study. Also representing these high schools were 665 full-time faculty members who carefully evaluated liberal arts courses in the areas of English, science, social studies, and mathematics.

All college and high school teachers possessed as a minimal requirement to evaluate courses — a Master's degree in one of four areas of specialization, namely, English, science, social studies, and mathematics. All instructors rated courses ONLY in their major area of teaching. All 1,065 college and high school teachers had to have at least four years of satisfactory teaching experience in order to participate in this study.

The sampling population, 269 colleges and universities and 520 secondary schools were contacted during 1965-66. The first contacts were made in January, 1965 through the use of opinionnaires.

Procedure

The general plan for the study was twofold, namely: (1) To enable 665 high school teachers of grades 11 and 12 the opportunity to examine sample outlines of courses ordinarily taught during the first two years of college in the areas of English, science, social studies, and mathematics and (2) To enable 400 college instructors the occasion to review high school level subjects as taught in grades 11 and 12 and specifically in the areas of English, science, social studies, and mathematics. In each area examined, both high school and college instructors reviewed the purpose, educational objectives, and a brief resume of the content of each course.

Of the 665 high school teachers, 160 evaluated 25 college English courses; 180 reviewed 25 social science courses; 150 analyzed 25 courses in mathematics, and 175 examined 30 college science courses. Some 105 college level courses were thus evaluated by secondary school teachers.

Of the 400 college faculty, 100 evaluated 25 high school English courses; 90 instructors examined 25 science courses; 110 faculty members analyzed 25 mathematic courses, and the remaining 100 college instructors reviewed 30 social science courses. The total number of courses subject to examination by college personnel numbered 105.

Arrangements included sending an opinionnaire to all participants which included courses of study. Teachers were asked the following:

IN REVIEWING THE COURSE OF STUDY,
CAN YOU FIND ANY DEGREE OF REPETITION
AS MAY BE RELATED TO THE COURSE(s) YOU TEACH?

All teachers used the following rating scale to judge the degree of repetition, if any, in the subject matter:

(PER CENT OF REPETITION)

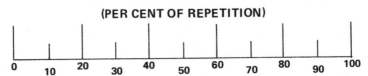

Note: If repetition is discerned, place a check mark (X) on the line above in the rating scale which may represent your opinion at this time.

Treatment of Data

The following tables at this point represent what the high school teachers thought of college level courses as far as repetition was concerned. For example, Table 3-1 indicates that the 160 high school teachers have estimated that slightly more than one-third (35.37%) of the *content* of English courses taught at the college level repeat has already been taught at the high school level. For example, nearly 28 per cent of the content of the college level course named *Fundamentals of Speech* is initially taught in high school; about 43 per cent of the content of *English Composition* taught at the college level is merely a repeat of what the student has already tackled in high school; 38 per cent of the content of *Appreciation of Poetry* is previously taught at the secondary level; 38 per cent of the content of *English Literature* has already been taught at the high school level and finally, 31 per cent of the content of the college course called *Advanced Creative writing* represents a duplication of the content taught at the secondary level.

TABLE 3-1
High School Teachers Rate Degree of Repetition of College Level Courses
Compared to Secondary School Courses

Area and Course	Number of Teachers Reporting (N = 160)	Number of Courses	Per Cent of Duplication		Standard Deviation (Sigma)
			Range	Mean	
ENGLISH					
Fundamentals of Speech.....	36	5	15-36	27.83	2.81
English Composition .	32	5	20-63	42.74	3.16
Appreciation of Poetry	28	5	18-54	38.41	2.73
English Literature...	30	5	20-52	38.25	2.58
Advanced Creative Writing	34	5	14-54	31.36	2.44
Combining all subjects, Mean =				35.37	2.74

Table 3-1 appears to indicate that slightly more than one-third (35.37%) of the content of college English surveys in this report is nothing more than a duplication of high school course work. Do these results indicate a statistically significant trend of opinion? To answer this question, all 160 high school teachers were asked to express their attitude toward the proposition: DO YOU BELIEVE THAT THE RATINGS YOU PREVIOUSLY MADE OF COLLEGE ENGLISH COURSES REFLECTS YOUR ATTI-TUDE WHICH WOULD PREVAIL TODAY? Teachers were queried to *underline* one of the following:

STRONGLY APPROVE - APPROVE - INDIFFERENT
DISAPPROVE - STRONGLY DISAPPROVE

The time lapse between the initial ratings and this follow-up study was 60 days. This design was adhered to so that data might be treated statistically using chi-square. With 4 df's and P's of 9.68 to 11.84 at the .05 and less levels, our chi-square test tends to show that our five groups of secondary school teachers really favor the proposition, hence their initial ratings may be stated to reflect a "statistically significant trend of opinion."

The results of English obtained in this report appear to confirm some earlier conclusions of a National Conference which was supported by the Cooperative Research Program of the United States Office of Education, and cosponsored by the *National Council of Teachers of English*. For example:

Fundamental changes in school English courses appear certain during the next few years. The two-year colleges, many of them connected administratively with the public schools, ought theoretically at least to be in closer touch with the reform movement than the four-year colleges and universities and able to profit from it sooner. And in fact, whether they wish it or not, the two-year colleges, and the others as well, will sooner or later find themselves obliged to revise their English programs in the freshman and sophomore years because of these pressures from below, as they are already being forced to modify their mathematics programs.[15]

It would be sensible to assess these reforms while there is still time, discover the ways and the degree to which they bear on later instruction, then make those changes that seem desirable. It is clearly better to plan intelligently for change than to be forced into it tardily and without foresight.[16]

TABLE 3-2
High School Teachers Rate Degree of Repetition of College Level Courses
Compared to Secondary School Courses

Area and Course	Number of Teachers Reporting (N = 180)	Number of Courses	Per Cent of Duplication		Standard Deviation (Sigma)
			Range	Mean	
SOCIAL SCIENCES					
The U.S. to 1865	40	5	25-60	45.63	3.47
The U.S. Since 1865	33	5	20-50	37.81	3.09
Civil War and Reconstruction	35	5	15-55	38.25	3.31
Sociology	34	5	20-57	40.16	3.52
Psychology	38	5	17-45	34.27	2.78
Combining all subjects, Mean =				39.35	3.23

Table 3-2 presents the results of the high school teachers evaluating the content of college level social science courses. The reader may note that slightly more than one-third (39.35%) of the content of the college social studies has already been taught in high school.

The U.S. to 1865 as taught in college duplicates roughly 46 per cent of the subject matter taught in high school; The U.S. Since 1865 college level course repeats some 38 per cent; Sociology is duplicated at 40 per cent and Psychology is reiterated 34 per cent.

Again, the writer was interested in discerning whether or not these results might indicate a statistical significant trend of opinion. Following the same procedure employed in English, the social science teachers (N=180) were administered the chi-square test using the earlier proposition stated for English personnel and levels of significance were at .05 and less thus indicating that the trend of thinking of these teachers was statistically significant.

Table 3-3, which follows, affords us the opportunity to review what some 175 high school teachers think of the content of science courses as taught at the college level and whether or not, this content is already presented at the high school level.

TABLE 3-3
High School Teachers Rate Degree of Repetition of College Level Courses
Compared to Secondary School Courses

Area and Course	Number of Teachers Reporting (N = 175)	Number of Courses	Per Cent of Duplication		Standard Deviation (Sigma)
			Range	Mean	
SCIENCE					
Physics.	35	6	15-35	27.34	2.71
Chemistry	30	6	10-28	22.56	1.83
Biology	37	6	14-43	29.28	3.14
Geology	34	6	10-24	18.31	1.69
Botany	39	6	10-32	23.47	1.25
Combining all subjects, Mean =				24.31	2.12

In reviewing Table 3-3, we find duplication for all courses reviewed by the secondary school teachers. Biology appears to lead the parade with some 29 per cent of the content already covered by the secondary school; Physics ranks second in repetition with 27 per cent; Botany ranks third with a 23 per cent; Chemistry ranks fourth at 22 per cent and Geology ranks last with 18 per cent of repetition.

If we combine all science subjects evaluated by the high school teachers, we find roughly 24 per cent of the content duplicates what is already taught at the high school level.

A chi-square test of the science teachers revealed levels of significance of .05 and less. Using the same proposition posed earlier for English teachers, we may regard the ratings by the high school science teachers as indicating a statistically significant trend of opinion.

TABLE 3-4
High School Teachers Rate Degree of Repetition of College Level Courses
Compared to Secondary School Courses

Area and Course	Number of Teachers Reporting (N = 175)	Number of Courses	Per Cent of Duplication Range	Mean	Standard Deviation (Sigma)
MATHEMATICS					
Algebra.	25	5	18-46	34.51	3.52
Geometry	35	5	15-37	27.63	2.41
Elementary Statistics . . .	30	5	8-22	17.42	1.79
Plane Trigonometry	24	5	10-25	18.97	1.94
Calculus I	36	5	5-20	13.25	2.08
Combining all subjects, Mean =				21.90	2.35

Reviewing Table 3-4 in the area of mathematics, one may note that the context of college *Algebra* is a repeat by the college of approximately 34 per cent of what has already been presented at the high school level; college *Geometry* duplicates about 28 per cent of what is taught in the curriculum of the secondary school; *Plane Trigonometry* is repeated some 18 per cent; *Elementary Statistics* overlaps some 17 per cent with high school level content and *Calculus I* is a duplicate of roughly 13 per cent.

If we combine the courses in mathematics, we find that slightly more than one-fifth, or 22 per cent of the content taught at the college level has already been covered at the high school.

A chi-square test of the 150 teachers of mathematics indicates .05 levels and less thus pointing to a statistically significant trend of opinion.

Reviewing Table 3-5, we find that colleges and universities are repeating slightly more than one-third, or 39 per cent of the content in *social science* courses which the college student has already been exposed to on the secondary level. The *social science* area apparently leads the parade as far as overlapping with high school courses. Next, in order of repetition, we find *English* at 35 per cent; *Science* at 24 per cent and least, *Mathematics* at 22 per cent.

TABLE 3-5
Summary: Rank Order of College Repetition of High School Courses

Course: Rank Order	Number of Teachers Reporting (N = 665)	Number of Courses	Per Cent of Duplication Range	Per Cent of Duplication Mean	Standard Deviation (Sigma)
1. Social Science	180	25	15-60	39.35	3.23
2. English	160	25	14-63	35.37	2.74
3. Science	175	36	10-43	24.31	2.12
4. Mathematics. .	150	25	5-46	21.90	2.35
Combining all subjects, Mean =				30.49	2.62

Combining all areas investigated, almost one-third, or 30 per cent of the content of all four areas of the college curriculum seem to be little more than high school courses rearranged into a college course and then offered under a new name, but *unmistakably* continuing as high school substance.

If we can assume that our findings are correct, that is, that nearly one-third, or 30 per cent of the content of college level courses are merely duplicates of secondary school subjects, we may look at this matter from another very important viewpoint — the financial status of the "duplicate student."

In the Fall of 1965, the number of enrollees in institutions of higher education totaled 3,999,940 and 1,967,471 for public and privately controlled institutions, respectively.[17] Tuition and required fees for the same period amounted to $222 and $831 for public and privately controlled institutions, respectively.[18] If nearly one-third of the content of subject matter taken during the first two years of college is merely a repetition of what the high school has already presented, an estimated 2,983,705 freshmen and sophomores enrolled in public and private institutions of higher education are paying tuition and required fees of $420,492,375 for course content that the student's parents have already reimbursed the state during the youths' secondary education role. The current academic year finds an increased enrollment in public and private institutions of higher education as well as increased tuition fees as compared with the school session of 1965-66. Therefore, the sum of

$420,492,375 may be considered but a minimal expenditure ALL parents will continue to pay for overlapping of subject matter on the collegiate level. This does not represent prudent economy in administering the programs in higher education in our country.

Several questions at this point are susceptible to close inspection and examination. For example:

1. Undoubtedly, some repetition of college subject-matter as related to the high school may be completely desirable and most welcome. The point is, WHO decides WHAT content of the secondary school should be repeated? If repetition is desirable, on what level should it begin and in what areas of the college curriculum? Is repetition based on students' needs and interests, or upon the college's aims and goals? How VALID and RELIABLE may the repetitious material be on the college level?

2. Overlapping of subject-matter should have a basic PURPOSE. What is the specific purpose of duplicating subject-matter on the college level when it has already been taught at the high school? If high schools knew the colleges' basic purpose, might it not assist high school personnel in providing better guidance and counseling services for high school youth?

3. Is it possible that one of the reasons why duplication of subject-matter exists is because the liberal arts college might be unaware of what is happening curricularwise at the secondary school level?

4. If institutions of higher education repeat what has been taught at the high school level, can this subject-matter be seriously labeled college subject-matter?

5. If colleges and universities throughout the country are using nearly one-third of the content of English, science, social studies, and mathematics as taught on the secondary school level, should these institutions continue to be called colleges and universities?

6. The *American Association of Colleges for Teacher Education* has cited: It is no overstatement that teacher preparation institutions are willing to certify persons prepared to teach who have but a small amount of knowledge and even less commitment to scholarly endeavor.[19] Since the college of liberal arts shares one-half the education of the prospective teacher, should not they also share this indictment of the *American Association of Colleges for Teacher Education* along with Schools of Education?

7. It is apparent from the results of this study that administrators and faculties of higher education and our secondary schools do NOT have a common understanding with respect to the goals to be sought in teaching.

8. Boards of Higher Education in the United States should trigger research activities in institutions of higher education so that both groups might be able to render enhanced commitments to educational functions of the state and nation which is based on reliable and factual bases of information.

College Personnel Evaluations

The first section of this study was devoted to reviewing the results of having high school teachers evaluate college level work taught during the first two years of college. This section of the study will find college instructors reviewing high school courses taught during the last two years of high school (grades 11 and 12). Is it possible that college personnel may react somewhat in the same manner as high school instructors?

TABLE 3-6
College Instructors Evaluate High School Courses to Ascertain
Possible Repetition as to Their College Courses

Area and Course	Number of Teachers Reporting (N = 100)	Number of Courses	Per Cent of Duplication		Standard Deviation (Sigma)
			Range	Mean	
ENGLISH					
English Literature...	20	5	15-30	23.49	1.83
American Literature...	20	5	10-25	18.06	1.97
Fundamentals of Speech.....	20	5	12-36	25.17	2.26
Journalism	20	5	10-40	27.58	2.84
Advanced Creative Writing	20	5	8-32	23.74	3.15
Combining all subjects, Mean =				23.61	2.41

Examining Table 3-6, we find that 28 per cent of the content of *Journalism* taught in high school is repeated again in college; 25 per cent of the content of *Fundamentals of Speech* taught at the secondary level is duplicated later in college; some 23 per cent of the content of *English Literature* overlaps in later college teaching;

24 per cent of the content of *Advanced Creative Writing* reappears later at the college level and finally, an estimated 18 per cent of the content of *American Literature* is taught again at the college level.

By combining all English subjects, we find roughly 24 per cent of the content of such courses being reiterated later during the first two years of college.

A chi-square test of the 100 college teachers 60 days later asking these teachers to express their attitude toward the proposition: DO YOU BELIEVE THAT THE RATINGS YOU PREVIOUSLY MADE OF_____COURSES REFLECTS YOUR ATTITUDE WHICH WOULD PREVAIL TODAY? Teachers were queried to *underline* one of the following:

STRONGLY APPROVE - APPROVE - INDIFFERENT
DISAPPROVE - STRONGLY DISAPPROVE

Chi-square indicted .05 and less levels of significance indicated that the attitude expressed by these faculty members toward repetition of English can be considered a statistically significant trend of opinion.

TABLE 3-7
College Instructors Evaluate High School Courses to Ascertain
Repetition as to Their College Courses

Area and Course	Number of Teachers Reporting (N = 100)	Number of Courses	Per Cent of Duplication		Standard Deviation (Sigma)
			Range	Mean	
SOCIAL SCIENCE					
Problems of American Democracy . .	20	6	5-40	29.13	2.64
Psychology	20	6	9-43	28.73	2.51
U.S. History . . .	20	6	5-45	26.26	2.60
Sociology	20	6	10-38	19.83	3.03
World History. . .	20	6	6-42	18.46	2.13
Combining all subjects, Mean =				24.48	2.58

Table 3-7 appears to indicate that 29 per cent of the content of *Problems of American Democracy* taught in high school is later duplicated at the college; 29 per cent of the content of high school *Psychology* later appears in college class work; 26 per cent of the content of *U.S. History* is duplicated later at college; 20 per cent of *Sociology* overlaps in college classes and finally, we find about 18 per cent of the content of *World History* is duplicated later in college.

By combining all *Social Science* courses, we find that nearly a quarter, or 24 per cent of the content of high school courses appears to be a regular inclusion of the college curriculum.

The chi-square test of 100 teachers indicated levels of significance at .05 and less thus pointing to the fact that the opinions earlier rendered by these college instructors appears to indicate a statistically significant trend of opinion.

In reviewing Table 3-8 which covers *Science* instruction at the secondary school level, one may note that 32 per cent of the content of *Chemistry* is repeated again in college level courses; 28 per cent of the content of *Physics* is later duplicated in college courses; about 24 per cent of the content of *Biology* is reiterated at the college level; 18 per cent of the content of *Botany* is reproduced later in college teaching and lastly, an estimated 14 per cent of the content of *Geology* reappears later in college courses.

By combining all Science courses as taught on the high school level (N = 25), we find that an estimated 23 per cent of the content of these courses are duplicated at the college level according to the college raters.

TABLE 3-8
College Instructors Evaluate High School Courses to Ascertain
Possible Repetition as to Their College Courses

Area and Course	Number of Teachers Reporting (N = 90)	Number of Courses	Per Cent of Duplication Range	Per Cent of Duplication Mean	Standard Deviation (Sigma)
SCIENCE					
Physics (PSSC)[20]	20	5	10-40	27.58	3.42
Chemistry (CHEM STUDY)[21] . .	20	5	15-45	32.41	3.61
Biology (BSCS)[22]	15	5	10-35	24.35	2.53
Geology	18	5	5-20	13.69	1.79
Botany	17	5	5-25	17.72	2.35
Combining all subjects, Mean =				23.47	2.74

Do these results indicate a statistically significant trend of opinion? According to the chi-square test, levels of significance of .05 and less are noted. Thus, the opinions of these raters may be regarded as statistically significant.

TABLE 3-9
College Instructors Evaluate High School Courses to Ascertain Possible Repetition as to Their College Courses

Area and Course	Number of Teachers Reporting (N = 110)	Number of Courses	Per Cent of Duplication		Standard Deviation (Sigma)
			Range	Mean	
MATHEMATICS					
UICSM[23]	25	5	10-35	24.51	2.84
SMSG[24]	20	5	5-40	25.63	3.13
Elementary Statistics . . .	20	5	10-25	19.84	1.75
Calculus I	20	5	10-30	22.37	2.98
Plane Trigonometry	25	5	5-28	17.45	3.26
Combining all subjects, Mean =				21.87	2.79

Table 3-9 indicates that some 17 per cent of the content of *Plane Trigonometry* taught in high school is later repeated in college; 24 per cent of the content of *UICSM* reappears later in college; some 26 per cent of *SMSG* as taught in the secondary school is duplicated later in college; 22 per cent of the content of *Calculus I* as taught in high school is later repeated in college and finally, some 20 per cent of *Elementary Statistics* content taught in high school is repeated in college.

Table 3-10 represents a summary of the four areas of high school subject-matter as reviewed by college personnel:

TABLE 3-10
Summary: Rank Order of High School Repetition of College Level Courses

Course: Bank Order	Number of Teachers Reporting (N = 400)	Number of Courses	Per Cent of Duplication		Standard Deviation (Sigma)
			Range	Mean	
1. Social Science	100	30	5-45	24.48	2.58
2. English	100	25	8-40	23.61	2.41
3. Science	90	25	5-45	23.47	2.74
4. Mathematics. .	110	25	5-40	21.87	2.79
Combining all subjects, Mean =				23.32	2.63

In reviewing Table 3-10, one may note that an estimated 23 per cent of the combined subjects already presented at the secondary school level undergoes repetition later at the college level.

It is indeed interesting to note that both Tables 3-5 and 3-10 indicate the rank order of subject-matter to be identical. Both high school instructors and college personnel rank *Social Science* subjects top priority as far as overlapping is concerned. *Mathematics* ranks last as compared with the other three disciplines.

Relationship between High School and College Evaluations

Since we have found a noticeable tendency for high school and college teachers to think somewhat similar relative to the subject-matter areas being duplicated on both levels, what might the coefficient of correlation reveal if we compare the ratings of both groups. Table 3-11 provides us with some idea of the strength of this relationship.

TABLE 3-11
Relationship between High School and College Personnel
Pertaining to Evaluating Subject-Matter

Area	N	r*	Standard Deviation	Level of Significance
English	100	.79	3.47	$< .001$
Science	90	.75	2.91	$< .001$
Social Science	100	.73	3.20	$< .001$
Mathematics	110	.68	2.65	$< .001$

*Mean r = (.74) using Fischer's z coefficient.

Table 3-11 indicates that the coefficients of correlation (Pearson r) extend from .68 to .79 with a mean r of .74. This .74 tends to suggest a moderately high relationship between the high school and college raters. And, this particular coefficient of correlation is significant at the $< .001$ level which permits us to assume that the results achieved in this bi-evaluation did not occur by chance alone.

Conclusions

1. If one compares the subjects (English, science, social studies, and mathematics) as taught on the college level during the first two

years with comparable courses taught in high school the last two years (grades 11 and 12), the degree of duplication is found to be a mean of 30.49 ± 2.63 per cent.

2. If one compares the subjects (English, science, social studies, and mathematics) as taught in high school (grades 11 and 12) with similar college level courses taught during the freshman and sophomore years, repetition is found to possess a mean of 23.32 + 2.63 per cent.

3. The mean per cent of duplication at the college level in rank order of importance shows *Social Science* the highest (39.35%); *English* (35.37%); *Science* (24.31%), and *Mathematics* (21.90%).

4. A chi-square of high school teachers (N = 665) some two months after rating college courses indicates that their evaluations can be considered a "statistically significant trend of opinion."

5. The mean per cent of overlapping at the high school level in rank order of importance shows *Social Science* the highest (24.48%); *English* (23.61%); *Science* (23.47%), and *Mathematics* (21.87%).

6. A chi-square of college instructors (N = 400) evaluating high school *English, Social Studies, Science*, and *Mathematics* courses some two months after they completed their initial ratings of these courses reveals that their initial judgments can be considered a "statistically significant trend of opinion."

7. In correlating high school teachers' ratings with college personnel ratings as related to duplication of subject-matter, we find *English* ranking the highest with an r of .79, *Science* with an r of .75, *Social Science* with an r of .73, and *Mathematics* revealing an r of .68. If we combine all subjects, our mean becomes an r of .74 which is significant at the < .001 level. Apparently, secondary and college level instructors exhibit a moderately high relationship when evaluating courses of instruction in their specialized areas of competency.

8. The overlapping of courses at both levels, namely high school and college, tends to suggest poor coordination and articulation between colleges of liberal arts and secondary schools throughout the country.

9. Since nearly one-third of the content of college teaching during the first two years represents a reiteration of what has already been taught at the secondary level, may this repetitive teaching actually be thwarting potential accomplishments in other

areas of the curriculum? Since our knowledge is expanding at a tremendous rate each year, can colleges afford to engage in this repetitive teaching technique? There are approximately 2100 institutions of higher learning of which more than 1500 prepare biloogy teachers that are certified to teach in secondary schools, yet most are not preparing biology teachers adequately, both in terms of biological concepts and in the process of science.[25]

10. The duplication of high school subject-matter at the college level cost students an estimated $420,492,375 for the 1965-66 academic session. Is this expenditure commensurate with what the college of liberal arts calls *quality teaching?* As a brief reminder, the parents of these college youth have already reimbursed the high schools in all states for the subject-matter duplicated at the college level. Is this repeat performance actually satisfying the GOALS of higher education? What documentary evidence do colleges of liberal arts possess to substantiate the need for this repetitive teaching?

Recommendations

1. Colleges of liberal arts should cooperatively address themselves to the secondary schools of this country relative to: How best may we work together to provide better sequence and articulation of courses of study?

2. Colleges of liberal arts should offer, at times convenient for college and secondary school personnel, opportunities consisting of seminars, workshops, conferences, inter-school visitation in order to aid and abet planning, development, analysis, and interpretation of curricular offerings in the hope that continuous and comprehensive evaluation will benefit the youth attending these schools.

3. State Departments of Education should provide guidelines to colleges and universities as to HOW both levels might coordinate their services. Appropriate consultant assistance should also be available from State Departments of Education. This level is particularly weak at the present time and needs to be strengthened.

4. The *basic* reason for the existence of administration is to facilitate instruction. Educational leadership at both the high school and college level may be seriously questioned. Professional

school and college level may be seriously questioned. Professional improvement of administrators needs to be *revitalized*. Administrators need to stress the inter-disciplinary approach to problems of a curricular nature. No single question is intensified primarily by its own boundaries. The parameter of any problem may balloon into many related disciplines.

5. A nationwide survey and analysis of actual inservice training practices and techniques introducing college and high school teachers and administrators to possible solutions, or ideas on how best to implement articulation of learning experiences should be a basic research proposal.

6. The NCTE, or *National Council of Teachers of English* and similar Councils for Science, Social Science, and Mathematics should insist and support research of an inter-disciplinary nature and assist in designing potential guideposts for colleges and secondary schools so that both levels may work together in joint-action as to what direction they might pursue best. Currently, both groups are comparable to a ship at sea without a rudder — just floundering.

7. Colleges of liberal arts need to reassess their testing programs. The need for appraising the educational growth of youth is vitally important. Testing in college needs to place more emphasis on the diagnostic ends: WHY did the student respond the way he did? These schools additionally need instruments of a predictive nature based on the curriculum coming under the colleges' control. The work - study - skills - habits - attitudes and appreciations of college youth should receive more attention; these, after all, are the FOUNDATION factors in all general learning situations.

8. The liberal arts college is currently being affected by two forces, namely: (1) The rapid development of the public community college which has already siphoned a large number of students who, it is presumed, would otherwise have enrolled in the liberal arts college. If this practice continues, the liberal arts college may have to limit its current four-year program to a two-year program beginning with the third year. And (2) The graduate professional schools are in the process of a downward extension and are planning and developing integrated programs of liberal arts and professional work beginning with the third year of college. If the two upper years become a part of the graduate school and the lower two years are taken over by the community junior college, where

does this leave the liberal arts college? It is quite possible that within a period of time, the liberal arts college may become practically nonexistent.

1Blanchard, B. Everard. *A National Survey: Curriculum Articulation between the College of Liberal Arts and the Secondary School.* A monograph. De Paul University, Graduate Programs Office, School of Education, Spring Quarter, 1971.

Paper presented to the *Middle States Association of Colleges and Secondary Schools*, Annual Meeting, Haddon Hall, Atlantic City, New Jersey, December, 1971; paper also presented to the *New England Association of Colleges and Secondary Schools*, Annual Meeting, Boston, Massachusetts, December, 1971. Both papers were reviews of *A National Survey, et al.*

2Benezet, Louis T., "Continuity and Change: The Need for Both," *The Future Academic Community.* Edited by John Caffrey, American Council on Education, Washington, D.C., 1969, p. 17.

3New York: McGraw-Hill Book Company.

4Garden City, N.Y.: Doubleday and Company.

5*Op. Cit.*, p. 24.

6Cowley, W.H. "Three Curricular Conflicts." *Liberal Education* 46: 467-83; December 1960.

7De Vane, William C. "A Time and a Place for Liberal Education." *Liberal Education* 50: 198-212; May 1964.

8Rudy, Willis. *The Evolving Liberal Arts Curriculum: A Historical Review of Basic Themes.* Publications of the Institute of Higher Education. New York: Bureau of Publications, Teachers College, Columbia University, 1960. 135 pp.

9McGrath, Earl J. *Memo to a College Faculty Member.* Publication of the Institute of Higher Education. New York: Bureau of Publications, Teachers College, Columbia University, 1961. 54 pp.

10McGrath, Earl J. "The College Curriculum — An Academic Waste-Land?" *Liberal Education* 49: 235-50; May 1963.

11Brinker, Paul A. "Our Illiberal Liberal-Arts Colleges: The Dangers of Undergraduate Overspecialization." *Journal of Higher Education* 31: 133-38; March 1960.

[12]Osburn, W.J. *Overlapping and Omissions in Our Courses of Study.* Bloomington, Illinois: Public School Publishing Company, 1928.

[13]Russell, John Dale and Judd, Charles H. *The American Educational System.* Chicago, Illinois: Houghton Mifflin Company, 1940. pp. 221-22.

[14]National Council for Accreditation of Teacher Education, *13th Annual List, 1966-1967,* 1750 Pennsylvania Avenue, N.W., Washington, D.C., 20006. Note: The *13th Annual List, 1966-1967* contains 449 colleges and universities.

[15]Archer, Jerome W., and Ferrell, Wilfred A. *Research and the Development of English Programs in the Junior College.* Cooperative Research Project No. X-004, National Council of Teachers of English, 1965, 508 South Sixth Street, Champaign, Illinois 61822. Page 2.

[16]*Ibid.,* pp. 2 and 3.

[17]*Standard Education Almanac.* Alvin Renetzky, Editor-in-Chief. Los Angeles, California: Academia Media, Inc., 1968, p. 286.

[18]*Ibid.,* p. 283.

[19]*Phi Delta Kappan.* Volume L, Number 9, May 1969, p. 547.

[20]*PSSC:* The Physical Science Study Committee started in 1956. Stresses the method on inquiry, uses laboratory work to enable students to work through experiments and make their own observations and conclusions.

[21]*CHEM STUDY:* Initiated in 1960 and extends prime importance to laboratory work. Students are taught to make their own discoveries, observations, and deductions.

[22]*BSCS:* Launched in 1959 and emphasizes three separate versions of the biological sciences, namely: the blue version, reportedly the most difficult, emphasizes biochemistry and physiology; the yellow version centers on genetics and the development of organisms; the green version focuses on evolution and ecology.

[23]*UICSM:* The University of Illinois Committee on Mathematics. Mathematical induction, sequences; elementary functions — powers, exponentials, and logarithms; circular functions and trigonometry; polynomial functions and complex numbers.

24*SMSG:* The School Mathematics Study Group. Grade 11, Intermediate Mathematics and Grade 12, Elementary Functions.

25*The Pre-Service Preparation of Secondary School Biology Teachers.* Addison E. Lee, Editor. Publication 25, *Commission on Undergraduate Education in the Biological Sciences* (CUEBS). Supported by a grant from the National Science Foundation to George Washington University, 1969, p. 3.

CHAPTER 4
A Comparative Analysis of Primary, Intermediate, Secondary, College and University Levels in Aptitude versus Achievement[1]

Introduction

Since World War II, our elementary and secondary schools throughout the country have improved their quality of teaching English, mathematics, science, social studies and reading.

Much of the last year of high school, in particular, is wasted for those already admitted to college. The students also come to college with more knowledge due to the influence of the higher levels of education of their parents and the easy availability of TV, books, and films. Many students are one year further advanced, academically, than their age group was at the end of World War II. The first year of college is often largely wasted for students with a better general background than that to which the colleges earlier adjusted and for students with clear academic or occupational goals.[2]

A National Survey: Curriculum Articulation between the College of Liberal Arts and the Secondary School[3] has indicated that the typical secondary youth of today is from two to four years advanced academically than his World War II predecessor.

Despite the fact that our high schools have been on the upgrade for the past decade or more with reference to improving the quality of instruction, an estimated six out of every ten students enrolling in college will fail to get the ultimate degree to which they aspire. The writer is concerned for a simple reason. It is exceedingly difficult to comprehend WHY entering freshmen who are so well trained academically in the basic disciplines on the secondary-school level fail to follow through toward satisfactorily completing degree requirements in the four-year college. The investigator is familiar with the dropouts due to finances, illness, low grade point averages, marriage, etc. The basic interest of the investigator is centered primarily on the academic habits, attitudes, under-standings, appreciations, and other related competencies associated with the learning process.

Purpose of Study

The basic purpose of this study was to ascertain the relationship between aptitude and achievement of primary, intermediate, high school, and college level youth.

What we are really interested in is whether or not the differences between the relationships are real differences or whether these relationships might be nothing more than chance variations. At this point, we follow the null hypothesis. Acceptance or rejection of the null hypothesis will be at the .01 level of significance.

Sampling Population

Questionnaires were forwarded to 300 elementary schools, 70 per cent responded; 400 high schools, 65 per cent responded; and 500 colleges and universities, 77 per cent responded. The questionnaires were mailed during January of 1965. On May 1, 1965 the reception of questionnaires ended and tabulation of data began. All schools were selected on a random basis from State Education Directories and from regional accreditation sources.

Approximately 4,375 students from 34 states comprised the subjects of this investigation. Of the 4,375 students, 1,850 represented public and private elementary schools; 1,200 were from public and private secondary schools, and the remaining 1,375 were college and university students. All public and private schools and institutions of higher education were regionally and fully accredited.

Colleges and universities reviewed in this investigation were both private and state supported. The investigator was interested in the first two undergraduate years of college (freshmen and sophomores). Specifically, the *college of liberal arts and sciences* is the primary subject.

Examples of such schools which were contacted by questionnaire might best be defined by extracting the data from the college or university catalog: for example —

AURORA COLLEGE IS, BY THE CHOICE OF ITS FOUNDING FATHERS AND THE CONTINUING CHOICE OF ITS PRESENT FACULTY AND ADMINISTRATION, A SMALL, CHRISTIAN, LIBERAL ARTS COLLEGE.[4]

Note: Aurora College is accredited by the North Central Association of Colleges and Secondary Schools.

THE PRIMARY EMPHASIS OF THE UNIVERSITY IS UPON UNDERGRADUATE EDUCATION IN THE LIBERAL ARTS AND SCIENCES.[5]

Note: Washington and Lee University is accredited by the Southern Association of Colleges and Schools.

EVERY FRESHMAN ENTERING THE UNIVERSITY IS ENROLLED IN THE UNIVERSITY COLLEGE. HE REMAINS A UNIVERSITY COLLEGE STUDENT UNTIL HE HAS COMPLETED AT LEAST 96 QUARTER CREDITS, INCLUDING THE WORK OF THE COLLEGE OF LIBERAL ARTS.[6]

Note: The principal accrediting organization applying to the University as a whole is the Southern Association of Colleges and Schools. More than 60 different regional and national education associations working in the various colleges, departments, and administrative offices of the University maintain accredited status and assist in promoting the highest possible educational standards. (Editor's note, p. 12).[7]

Procedure

Each student possessed two variables which might be correlated to determine the existing relationship: for example, the *first* variable we will call the "input" factor as determined by a student's score on a standardized aptitude test. The *second* variable we will term the "output" factor as measured by the student's grade point average at the termination of each academic year.

The unreliability of teacher's marks is known, but since grade point averages are used to promote students, to gain entrance to honor's programs, to retain students in the same grade level, etc., it is utilized in this study on the same reference plane.

The "input" or aptitude level of all students was taken from the official cumulative record or unofficial transcript of credits. The various tests used were: *The California Test of Mental Maturity; Cooperative School and College Ability Tests; Henmon-Nelson Tests of Mental Ability; Kuhlmann-Anderson Intelligence Tests; Lorge-Thorndike Intelligence Tests; Otis Quick-Storing Mental Ability Tests; Ohio State University Psychological Test; SRA Tests of General Ability; Terman-McNemar Test of Mental Ability and the Illinois Index of Scholastic Aptitude.*[8]

Discussion

The efficiency of a school system is sometimes determined by the manner in which students apply themselves to the program of subjects and activities. Although it is extremely difficult to obtain a reliable source indicative of such efficiency, the data is listed in Table 4-1 reveals roughly the extent to which students approach their capacity to work as evaluated by school marks.

TABLE 4-1
Capacity to Learn versus Quality of Achievement

Level	Grade	Number of Students	Correlation Coefficients	Level of Significance
Primary School	1 - 3	1000	.81	$\leq .001$
Intermediate School	4 - 6	850	.70	$\leq .001$
High School	9 - 12	1200	.62	$\leq .001$
College	13 - 14	1325	.51	$\leq .001$

Conclusions

The inferences as might be drawn from Table 4-1 appear to indicate that children in the *primary grades* make the *greatest use* of their *ability to learn*, whereas *college students make the least*. Each of the correlation coefficients are significant at the $\leq .001$ level of significance. We hereby reject the null hypothesis as it meets the level criterion as originally set by the investigator.

In spite of the lack of reliability of school marks, they do represent the most tangible means available at the moment for studying many vital school problems.

Implications

The probably inferences as might be drawn from this study are listed under five headings, namely: (1) Administration and Faculty; (2) Curriculum; (3) Evaluation; (4) Research and (5) Accreditation.

Administration and Faculty

1. Is it possible that at the administrative level (Presidents, Deans, Chairmen, etc.) that the appointed candidates may NOT be adequately qualified to handle the responsibilities placed upon them? If the basic PURPOSE of administration is to facilitate instruction, a deficiency of meaningful administration is apparent in this report.

2. If the preferred goal systems of administrators and faculty contrast sharply, and if administrators are in a position to impose their preferences on the faculty, is it possible that the climate ensuing might directly affect faculty teaching as well as student performance?

3. Is it possible that many college and university instructors are inadequately prepared in the subject-matter they teach? For example, the textbook specialist just fresh from Exterior University with his Ph.D., lacks any teaching experience whatsoever, but did complete a dissertation which is widely read, "The Structural Relationships of Pteridophytes and the Germination Power of the Radish Seed." This candidate is teaching undergraduate and graduate students in the area of education. Is this practice to be condoned?

Curriculum

1. Since the parameters of GENERAL EDUCATION have never been scientifically investigated, nor adequately defined for students

who may plan to enter degree programs, WHY have such course content as a prerequisite to matriculate in degree programs?

2. Since the modern college curriculum is addicted to fragmentation, inflation and proliferation of courses and content, is it possible that such an existing condition might trigger a lack of motivational challenge to the student?

3. Is it possible that the lack of proper sequence and articulation between institutions of higher education and secondary schools may be a crucial variable for college students not working up to capacity?

Evaluation

1. Apparently, evaluation is being slighted in institutions of higher education. If adequate techniques were utilized, colleges and universities would have a sound basis for making value judgments because institutions of higher education would be concerned with a student's abilities and progress.

Research

1. Many teachers have little or no knowledge of the research that has been done in their field and are unaware that there are practical findings that could be applied to their everyday work.

2. Research is an integral part of the instructional program. Better understanding of problems and basic issues will result from carefully designed research proposals. If research results are not properly disseminated, then we cannot expect practitioners to utilize even the most significant and competent studies.

Accreditation

1. Is it possible that accreditation associations might deal as specifically with colleges and universities as they do with secondary schools? For example, consistency of accrediting philosophies and practices should be emphasized.

2. The reactions of the seven regional accrediting commissions and especially of their professional staff members to the study group report provide strong indications that institutional accreditation truly stands at the threshold of major changes and improvement.[9]

[1]Blanchard, B. Everard. De Paul University, Graduate Programs Office, School of Education, Third Interim Report, Winter Quarter, 1971.

[2]Less Time, More Options, Education Beyond The High School, A Special Report and Recommendations by *The Carnegie Commission on Higher Education*, New York: McGraw-Hill Book Company, January, 1971. p. 7.

[3]Blanchard, B. Everard. De Paul University, Graduate Programs Office, School of Education, Second Interim Report, Spring Quarter, 1971.

[4]Aurora College Catalog, Aurora, Illinois, 1968-1970, p. 5.

[5]Washington and Lee University, General Catalogue, Lexington, Virginia, 1968-1969, p. 9. (General Information.)

[6]The University of Tennessee, General Catalog, Knoxville, Tennessee, 1966-1968, p. 198.

[7]*Ibid.*, p. 12.

[8]The ten aptitude tests as listed were used because of the different standardized testing programs administered by school officials. Conversion of correlations were carried out by resorting to the use of Fischer's z technique.

The *Illinois Index of Scholastic Aptitude* is a test devised by the investigator to replace the current I.Q. test. It is published and distributed by Western Psychological Services, 12031 Wilshire Boulevard, Los Angeles, California. 90025.

[9]*Federation of Regional Accrediting Commissions of Higher Education*, "A Report on Institutional Accreditation in Higher Education," Recommendations of the Council of the Federation Regarding Institutional Accreditation, 5454 South Shore Drive, Chicago, Illinois 60615, November 1970, p. 23.

✿
CHAPTER 5
The Elementary School

AMONG *The Ten Most Significant Educational Research Findings In The Past Ten Years*, Daniel Griffiths, Associate Dean of the School of Education, New York University, included Benjamin S. Bloom's *Stability and Change in Human Characteristics* in which Bloom inquires into the quantitative development of human characteristics.

Bloom's review of almost 1,000 studies hypothesizes that, "the environment in which the individual develops will have its greatest effect on a specific characteristic in its most rapid period of change and will have least effect on the characterized in its least rapid period of growth.[1]

Dean Griffith sees the impact of Bloom's work in the mushrooming interest in early education, and reflected in such programs as Head Start, Nursery School and kindergarten education. He suggests that:

> The research on human characteristics is very probably the most significant line of inquiry in the past ten years, and it has implications for all aspects of the educational system.[2]

Psychologist Benjamin S. Bloom estimates that about 50 per cent of mature intelligence is developed by age four and another 30 per cent by age eight. Some psychologists doubt whether any amount of remedial work later on will enable a child to develop intellectually to his full potential if he does not receive the proper stimulation at the proper time — that is, very young. While there is disagreement as to the optimum time for beginning systematic learning, there is general agreement that it has been a mistake to leave the intellectual development of young children almost entirely to chance.[3]

Increasing pressures during the past decade have brought about a downward movement of courses in the curriculum. Advanced skills and special training, previously reserved for junior and senior high school education, have been introduced into the elementary time block of common learnings. The formal teaching of foreign languages, basic principles of economics, and advanced principles of mathematics are now introduced to the student at an earlier age. Even industrial arts, or vocational education which was primarily a secondary school subject some two decades ago, is currently taught in the elementary school.

Two facts, namely: (1) The mental maturity of a child at eight years of age reaching 80 per cent of his total plus (2) The downward extension of courses into the elementary school necessitates a *revised structuring* of the elementary level. Since foundational training is indispensable, the elementary structure proposed by the writer would look as illustrated in Figure 5-1:

FIGURE 5-1: Proposed Elementary School Structure

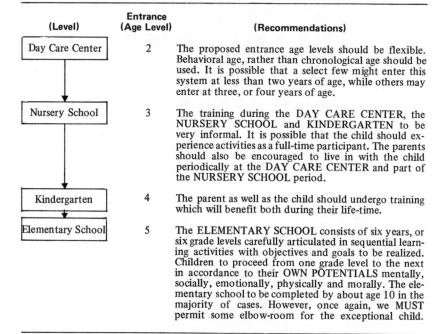

(Level)	Entrance (Age Level)	(Recommendations)
Day Care Center	2	The proposed entrance age levels should be flexible. Behavioral age, rather than chronological age should be used. It is possible that a select few might enter this system at less than two years of age, while others may enter at three, or four years of age.
Nursery School	3	The training during the DAY CARE CENTER, the NURSERY SCHOOL and KINDERGARTEN to be very informal. It is possible that the child should experience activities as a full-time participant. The parents should also be encouraged to live in with the child periodically at the DAY CARE CENTER and part of the NURSERY SCHOOL period.
Kindergarten	4	The parent as well as the child should undergo training which will benefit both during their life-time.
Elementary School	5	The ELEMENTARY SCHOOL consists of six years, or six grade levels carefully articulated in sequential learning activities with objectives and goals to be realized. Children to proceed from one grade level to the next in accordance to their OWN POTENTIALS mentally, socially, emotionally, physically and morally. The elementary school to be completed by about age 10 in the majority of cases. However, once again, we MUST permit some elbow-room for the exceptional child.

Day Care Centers

At the 1970 White House Conference on Children, delegates representing various women's groups were among the most vocal in their demands that child care be made available around the clock throughout the year for all who want it, not just for indigent or minority groups. Such delegates also vehemently urged that federally supported day care be completely divorced from public assistance — thus officially removing the taint of social pathology from day-care services.[4]

Despite the importance of these developments, however, the most fundamental influence has been the steady flow of information about the importance of the early childhood years. Evidence has gradually accumulated that certain kinds of experiences during the early years greatly influence how a child grows up in a society. Although the data are based on only about 10 years of research, the results have filtered out from scientific laboratories to popular magazines and thence to parents of all social classes, and the result is that parents are clamoring for more such programs for their children. As many of these same parents need child care, the request is generally for day care rather than "early education" per se.[5]

Day care can no more be separated from education than it can from welfare or health. Florence Ruderman in her book *Child Care and Working Mothers* had this to say: Day care, regardless of the auspices under which it is offered, should be developed as a child-care program; a program directed to optimum social and psychological health of the young child whose mother cannot care for him some part of the day . . . But a given family's need for social carework or other forms of help should no more define day care, nor determine eligibility for it, than the existence of social science departments in schools and hospitals now defines these facilities as social work services. For organized child-care service in this country to develop and meet adequately a growing social need, it must be recognized as a positive social institution and enabled to stand in its own right as an essential child-care program.[6]

At this moment in history, when we are on the threshold of embarking on a nationwise program of social intervention offered through comprehensive child care, we let ourselves prattle about such things as cost per child, physical facilities, or even community control. And when we begin to think big about what

kinds of children we want to have in the next generation, about
which human characteristics will stand them in good stead in a
world changing so rapidly, we fall back on generalities such as care
and protection. Yet any social institution that can shape behavior
and help instill values and competencies and life-styles should also
shape policy. Early child care is a powerful instrument for
influencing patterns of development and the quality of life for
children and adults. Because of its power, those who give it
direction must not think or act with timidity.[7]

If we were to disregard the differing conceptual definitions of day
care and education, we would be left with a practical explanation
for their historical development along different tracks. Namely, day
care has traditionally served the child younger than five or six while,
historically, public education has not assumed a major role before
this age.

However, during the past 10 years, the rapid growth in our
knowledge of children's early intellectual development has revealed
the great importance of the early years of life for the acquisition of
knowledge and problem-solving skills. Research has completely
invalidated any concept of education as a process that suddenly
begins at a child's fifth or sixth birthday. Since practical realities
usually mandate complete and continuous supervision of young
children, early education must frequently be linked with day care if
it is to be possible at all.[8]

A meaningful linkage between day care and education can help
to penetrate these organizational boundaries by conceptualizing the
educational task as sharing in the socialization process from
adolescence.

A working example is the Kramer School in Little Rock, Arkansas,
site of the University of Arkansas' Center for Early Development and
Education. Here exists one of the few elementary schools in the
United States in which infants, toddlers, and preschoolers enjoy their
share of the building and the campus. Children ranging in age from
one to 13 or 14 years share breakfast in the school cafeteria in the
morning and play on the grounds after school. Big ones help little
ones; younger children use older children as models. Kramer is an
"extended day school" where any child in attendance who needs
day care, between 7 a.m. and 5 p.m., may find it. Many communities
could duplicate this workable model of day care and education
blending comfortably and naturally in a public school setting.[9]

Another effect of integrating day care and the schooling process would be the relaxation of arbitrary time schedules. There is probably nothing more rigid and tyrannical in our school operation than the daily schedule. Like the preacher in Ecclesiastes, we seem to feel there is a time to arrive, a time to eat breakfast, a time to read, a time to learn math, a time to have recess, and — above all, a time to go home.[10]

One of the greatest concerns currently being voiced is that day care will weaken the tie between parents and children, particularly if the service is made universally available for very young children.

If day care can defuse the myth about the amount of time children must participate in order to "adjust" or "benefit" from the program, both children and families would benefit. For example, in discussions of whether infant day care is good or harmful, we tend to limit the debate to the full day care context. Why can't we have, instead, a one-hour program for infants in which they would receive special teaching, preferably in the company of their own mothers?[11]

Linking day care and education would facilitate the fullest utilization of property. Although full year and full day utilization of school property is hopefully on the rise, school buildings continue to be under utilized by the public which owns them. A combination of education and day care would automatically increase the utilization of school property with important implications for the design of buildings. For example, more space might be needed for activities such as arts, crafts, and gymnastics. In the design of buildings to be used for a long day, there will need to be areas in which a child can have some privacy and feel comfortably alone. Space for parent activities would also have to be considered.[12]

With the educative-protection orientation of child caring institutions, alternatives to the elementary-early childhood programs bear consideration. For example, early childhood day care programs could be located in or near junior high or high schools. In such a pattern, adolescents could utilize the day care facilities as laboratories for learning about child care and for acquiring skills in working with young children; teenagers could help the family by accompanying the younger to and from the school setting.[13]

A day care center affiliated with an institution of higher education preparing young people for teacher education at the elementary or preschool level would offer excellent opportunities to the prospective teacher as to the varied implications involved in the learning process. Such clinical experience would be equivalent to the internship and residency of young men studying to be physicians and surgeons in medicine.

If such examples as portrayed can become a reality, the home and the school can work more cooperatively and efficiently in the child-rearing task. Ideally, the all-day care centers for children of three to five years should be organized to provide the combination of an educational program for part of the day and home-like care for the remainder.

Parent Education: Children Under Three Years

Most of the leading scholars believe that age three is early enough to introduce children to formal schooling. They believe that there is insufficient knowledge about infant development to have formal education for them outside the home. For this reason programs for the education of parents to serve as "teachers" of those young children is the safest and most promising action until much more research is done.[14]

These programs are scattered throughout the country on an experimental basis. Experience suggests that they should be variable to meet the needs of parents. Some with little educational background will need a minimum training of two or three hours each week for several weeks. They would be taught how to work with their children in selected learning episodes involving language skills, positive reinforcements of particular behaviors, concept formation, and perceptual acuity. After an initial course of instruction there would be follow-up observations and conferences.[15]

The parents would follow a program of spending a few minutes each day with the child following prescribed activities. The supervisor would confer at regular intervals with the parent for evaluation of progress and planning further activity. These actions would be supplemented by written materials.[16]

Nursery Schools: Three and Four Years

At age three most children are mature enough to function well in small groups. They are becoming independent in caring for themselves — tying shoe laces, buttoning coats, washing hands, and toileting. Gross motor coordination is becoming distinctive for total body movement and balance as seen in climbing, running, and active group play. Fine motor coordination is observed in ability to use small objects such as crayons, paint brushes, and scissors.[17]

Cognitive development also is becoming distinctive. Many children at three years of age have a vocabulary of one thousand words or more, with a high degree of comprehension. Average sentence length is about five or six words. Their speech-sound discrimination ranges from 25 per cent to 75 per cent accurate. They are taking on adult language patterns of articulation. Problem-solving is still largely trial and error. They are showing evidence of learning how to learn. Conceptual development is in a distinctive stage.[18]

These characteristics suggest that children at three years of age are ready for an environment that is planned for proper stimulation and challenge, for creativity and satisfaction. The nursery school can provide that environment under guidance of skillful and professional personnel with proper space and materials.[19]

A brief image of the nursery school would be as follows: An instructional unit would consist of fifteen to twenty children, all of one age or a mixture of three- and four-year olds. The staff would consist of a teacher and two aides, supplemented by a mother on a rotating basis among all the parents of the children in the class. The length of the school day for the children should be from two and one-half to three hours for five days each week.

The indoor space should consist of 1,500 to 2,000 square feet for a group of fifteen to twenty children. The room should be divided into five or six activity areas: (1) reading and listening; (2) manipulative activities with large objects such as building blocks and toys; (3) manipulative activities with small objects such as puzzles, nesting cups, and peg boards; (4) science activities such as aquaria, small animal cages, rock collections, plants, and others; (5) housekeeping activities with dolls, doll houses, and simple tools; (6) dining area for snacks and lunch; (7) art activities with paper, scissors, and paints; (8) open space for activity of the total class.

The room should have auxiliary space for storage of heavy clothing, toilet facilities, sink facilities for washing hands, and a storage area for supplies and equipment. In addition, there should be outdoor space of about 2,000 square feet of play area specially equipped and designed for children of ages three and four.

These basic characteristics of the physical environment suggest a highly flexible program that is designed for the children. Activity would consist of individual and small group work (or play) throughout the day with exception of snacks, lunch, and group singing. Much of the time would be spent in activities with three to five members. About half of the day would be spent in activities chosen freely by the children.

The total program is designed to develop speech, language articulation, problem-solving, self-image, and other cognitive qualities. In addition there is attention to social and physical development. There is opportunity for free exploration in activities suitable to the children, such as playing at cooking, listening to music and stories, and building various structures. Each child can set his own pace, staying with an activity as long as he likes. There are self-correcting activities. For example, an auto-tutor will operate only if the child learns the proper manipulation. He has time to discover many things for himself.[20]

Good days for children this age are happy and full of stimulating new experiences in a wider world where teachers continually answer the "why's." Both affective and cognitive development are furthered.

Kindergarten Years

The basic image of the kindergarten is similar to the nursery school with certain exceptions. The children are older and thus the program is structured to accommodate their greater maturity. An adequate instructional unit would consist of a teacher, a teacher intern, and an aide (or two aides), supplemented by a volunteer mother for twenty to twenty-five children. The amount of space should be from 2,000 to 2,500 square feet with five or six activity areas for language arts, science, art activities, symbolic play for building objects with blocks and construction sets, use of small tools such as scissors, hammers, screwdrivers, toy animals, and a host of others.

The school session should be from three to three and one-half hours per day with a program that has variable activity, but somewhat more formally structured than the nursery school. Instruction in the basic skills of language arts, mathematics, science, and other areas is organized in small groups for individual activity with learning materials, and skilled guidance for pupil-to-pupil interaction. The complexity of learning activity is in keeping with the maturity of the children.

Programs for involvement of parents should continue through kindergarten and into the elementary grades. Their nature may change but they serve a continuing function of fundamental need.

The teacher should have only one session per day. After children are dismissed the teacher and her assistants should have time to evaluate their work and to plan ahead. They should have time to work with parents on evaluation of pupils' progress and to plan activities.[21]

The Elementary School

As indicated in Figure 5-1, Proposed Elementary School Structure, the reader will note that this elementary system is composed of four levels, namely: (1) Day Care Center; (2) Nursery School; (3) Kindergarten and (4) Elementary School. Parent education is also an important aspect of this system and stress should be keyed to this *cooperative* endeavor between the home and the school at all times.

McLure and Pence[22] have outlined the most critical characteristics peculiar to the modern elementary school, namely:

1. The staff is committed to total school change rather than piece-meal revisions by a few teachers.

2. Change is based on a systematic plan of study and action by the entire staff.

3. The educational plan involves participation of citizens and approval of local educational authorities.

4. The plan has formulated objectives, phases of development, and provisions for periodic evaluation and revisions.

5. The program emphasizes breadth and richness of experience for every child.

6. Instruction requires a high degree of collaboration of staff members. There is a variety of instructional grouping with much emphasis on individualized study and pacing of work. Variable phasing and grouping are substitutes for the traditional grades.

7. Pupils with special needs have access to a greater number of staff members for assistance. Thus, special programs have become

more integrated and stronger than in the traditional "self-contained" classes.

8. The traditional libraries are expanded into complex learning centers, combining all learning resources.

9. The physical environment is designed to accommodate an open type program. Instructional areas are clustered for team and group teaching, special rooms for variable size groups and activities. Each of these schools has a new plant with space that is designed to fit the general concept of the new program.

10. The schools have more than the usual amount and variety of instructional equipment and supplies.

The whole experience in young children is strategic in a child's personal development and in his educational process. The child learns through play and through play he seeks and finds his own identity. He finds out what he can do successfully and what he cannot do without help. He learns how to make friends and how to enjoy them. He learns about his own place in the family, in the classroom, the school at large, and through this process he ultimately learns his own place and role in society. Above all, the child is an individual in his own right, and he must have the time and opportunity to find his own value as a human being and to determine his own moral values. He must have time to grow. It is not a process that can be hurried, nor is there any phase in the growth continuum of which he can be cheated, without injury.[23]

This plan of education as illustrated by the writer is a phenomenon which millions of children likely will become a vital part by the year 2000. The list of challenges which face us and our schools is endless. There are two ways to meet these challenges. One is to continue as we have been doing — to ignore them and spend our time, energy and money on military hardware and permanently putting a man on the moon to control outer space stations, meanwhile wringing our hands over the delinquency, crime and mental instability which are the consequences of an undernourished educational system. The other is to spend more time, energy and money to give every child in this country the kind of education that is needed to bring out his highest potentialities.

As Dr. James E. Allen stated in an address:[24]

> If we analyze our plans for education, we shall find that
> most of them are still developed in terms of assumptions

that we have long accepted as the basis of our educational system. Many of these assumptions are no longer tenable as we look ahead to education as a function much broader than the traditional school and classroom. A new degree of cooperation and interaction will be required, and this cannot be achieved if we continue to approach policy making and the support of education from a narrow, personal or group-interest point of view.

The writer is highly optimistic concerning the future role of this proposed elementary educational ladder for American youth.

There is every indication of a gradual movement toward the varied levels of education as proposed by the author. This type of education should be the prerogative of every child as this plan provides a thorough grounding in the fundamentals.

---

[1]Griffith, Daniel, "The Ten Most Significant Educational Research Findings of the Past Ten Years," *SRIS Quarterly*, A Publication of Phi Delta Kappa's School Research Information Service, Vol. 1, No. 2, Spring 1968, p. 23.

[2]*Ibid.*, p. 23.

[3]*Carnegie Quarterly*, Carnegie Corporation of New York, Vol. XVII, No. 1, Winter 1969, p. 1.

[4]Caldwell, Bettye M., "A Timid Giant Grows Bolder," *Saturday Review*, February 20, 1971, p. 48.

[5]*Ibid.*, p. 48.

[6]*Ibid.*, p. 66.

[7]*Ibid.*, p. 66.

[8]Caldwell, Bettye M., "Day Care: Pariah to Prodigy," *Bulletin, American Association of Colleges For Teacher Education*, Vol. XXIV, No. 2, April 1971, p. 1.

[9]*Ibid.*, p. 4.

[10]*Ibid.*, p. 4.

[11]*Ibid.*, p. 4.

[12]*Ibid.*, pp. 4-5.

[13]*Ibid.*, p. 5.

[14]McLure, William P., and Pence, Audra May. *Early Childhood and Basic Elementary and Secondary Education: Programs,*

Demands, Costs. National Educational Finance Project. Special Study No. 1. Bureau of Educational Research, College of Education, University of Illinois at Urbana-Champaign, 1970, p. 20.

[15]*Ibid.*, p. 20.

[16]*Ibid.*, pp. 20-21.

[17]*Ibid.*, p. 22.

[18]*Ibid.*, p. '22.

[19]*Ibid.*, p. 22.

[20]*Ibid.*, pp. 22-23.

[21]*Ibid.*, pp. 24-25.

[22]*Op. Cit.*, p. 1.

[23]Rothman, Esther and Levine, Madeline, "From Little League to Ivy League — With a Dash of Math and Science in Between," *The Educational Forum*, Vol. XXVIII, No. 1, November 1963, pp. 32-33.

[24]Allen, Jr., James E., "Needed: A New Point of View," *Educational Record*, Vol. 52, No. 2, Spring 1971, p. 151. (Lecturer in education and public affairs at Princeton University, at the convention of the American Association of School Administrators, 22 February 1971 in Atlantic City.)

❧
CHAPTER 6
The Secondary School

WE ARE slowly thinking our way through a thicket of bitter disappointment and humiliating truth to the realization that a twentieth century educational philosophy is as hopelessly outdated today as the horse and buggy. Automation and technology have already exercised an initial influence on secondary school students; curriculum reorganization is underway; new teaching methods are being introduced; teacher education is being seriously questioned and students are faced with the need of adapting their educational training to the specific needs of the business and the industrial world.

In Chapter 5, the writer proposed a system of elementary education which concerns four vitally important stages, namely: (1) Day Care Center; (2) Nursery School; (3) Kindergarten and (4) Elementary School, grades 1 through 6.

Grades 7 and 8 traditionally have most often been labeled the last two years of the elementary school, or in some states, grades 7 and 8 have been called the junior high school. At any rate, the writer suggests that grades 7 and 8 NOW become the first two years of high school and what is presently the freshman and sophomore year, or grades 9 and 10 in high school, would NOW become the LAST two years of high school. In other words, a new structure is suggested. Figure 6-1 portrays this reorganizational pattern.

FIGURE 6-1
The New High School Structure

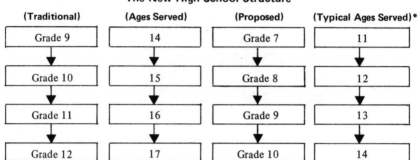

(Traditional)	(Ages Served)	(Proposed)	(Typical Ages Served)*
Grade 9	14	Grade 7	11
Grade 10	15	Grade 8	12
Grade 11	16	Grade 9	13
Grade 12	17	Grade 10	14

*Obviously, these age levels must make some provisions for the exceptional student. Flexibility, therefore, would prevail in all instances.

As the reader may note, the secondary school as proposed would decrease the age level of graduation from high school by approximately three years; that is, in lieu of graduating at the age of 17 or 18, a student might complete all required work by the age of 14 or 15. It is quite possible that a select few might complete all high school requirements prior to the age of 14, or a student may desire to take a little longer and graduate at the age of 16, 17, or more, pending upon circumstances.

The most common minimum age for compulsory "school attendance" is seven years and the most prevalent maximum age is sixteen years. Utilizing this proposed secondary school structure would automatically eliminate the "current drop-out" which usually occurs at age sixteen.

Can this new structure be justified? The writer believes that this question can be answered in the affirmative. By ALL means YES. There are several reliable research projects which tend to sanction the author's belief. For example, Bloom[1] has stated that "by age 9 (grade three) at least 50 per cent of the general achievement pattern at age 18 (grade twelve) has been developed, whereas at least 75 percent of the pattern has been developed by about age 13 (grade seven)." In brief, these figures, if acceptable, show that three-fourths of a child's growth in achievement has occurred prior to adolescence. As a corollary to his understanding that early development is highly important, Bloom has asserted that the more stable a characteristic becomes the more effort is needed to change it. Thus it would seem that the job of compensatory education in high school with adolescents will take more effort than will compensatory provisions at the lower levels. While offering some hope for significant gains for those who work with adolescents, the essence of this study is that the battle is largely won or lost before a child ever reaches high school.

The Carnegie Commission on Higher Education has stated:[2] *Young people have changed.* They reach physiological and social maturity at an earlier age — perhaps by one year, and yet more of them are kept longer in the dependent status of a student. They are more resistant to the seemingly endless academic "grind" that, for more of them, goes on for more and more years without letup, sitting at their desks as recipients of knowledge but without productive contribution.

The National Survey by the writer[3] has indicated that the college level courses as taught in the social sciences repeat some 39.35 percent of the course content already taught on the secondary school level; some 35.37 percent of the content of English at the college level has already been acquired by the student while he attended high school; science course content is repeated an estimated 24.31 percent and mathematics is duplicated at the college level approximately 21.90 percent. This study tends to suggest that high school students today are from two to four years advanced academically vis-a-vis their World War II predecessors. What this means is that we may find in our modern secondary school today, students at the third year (juniors) engaging in the same work academically as the college and university student who is enrolled in the sophomore year of study.

In another study titled, *A Comparative Analysis of Primary, Intermediate, Secondary, College and University Levels of Aptitude Versus Achievement*[4] the author found that children in the primary grades make the greatest use of their ability to learn, whereas college students make the least use of their ability to learn. The difference between the mean correlation of .62 for high school students and the mean correlation for college students which was .51 can be taken as real and dependable as the critical ratio of 3.26 permits us to be taken as real and dependable as the critical ratio of 3.26 permits us to accept the superiority of high school students versus college students. In other words, the critical ratio (CR) indicates that a statistically significant difference exists between secondary and college youth which favors the former over the latter.

These findings appear to supplement and reinforce the idea that America needs to implement a reorganization of structure in the framework of the educational system coupled with a reassessment of subjects currently being taught in our secondary schools and colleges.

The wise men of whom we have generally agreed that the principles upon which education was conducted up to a century ago fulfilled well the limited objectives of that earlier era. Were we living today in one of the many societies in which they lived, we might follow their consensus with confidence. But we are not. We are living in a society which none of these men of imagination ever imagined.

As McLure and Pence point out in their special study, *Early Childhood and Basic Elementary and Secondary Education*,[5] there is common agreement in the literature and in the field that secondary education should change substantially during the 1970s. Some extremists impatiently call for a revolution in purposes, structures, processes, and allocation of resources. These seem to be few in number, at least those who have expressed their views in print. No respondents in this study could be classified as advocating a continuation of the status quo. All of them estimate the needs to be in excess of realistic accomplishments.

In projecting a potential image of the schools in the 1980's, six characteristics appear to emerge, namely:

1. THE PROCESS OF DECISION-MAKING. There is something unique about the attention given to educational objectives. They have become a subject of regular study, evaluation, and revision. Decisions on major innovative changes occur after exhaustive study, wide involvement of the community, and strong leadership by the school.
2. THE EDUCATIONAL PROGRAM. The program is distinctive for its relation to objectives and its breadth of curriculum. Much of the staff effort is devoted to evaluation of the learning materials and revision of content.
3. THE STRUCTURE OF THE EDUCATIONAL PROCESS. The schedule of activity is more flexible than the traditional school. It varies to accommodate differentiated sizes of

instructional groups, and to provide time and attractive settings for independent study.

4. THE STAFF. Specialization, division of labor, and collaborative activity are characteristics on which these schools are distinguished from the typical ones. There are some teacher aides but numerically fewer than in the elementary schools. The climate of the school is distinctive for its commitment as a responsibility of the total staff as well as of individuals. The staff spends less energy on student discipline because the environment is conducive to greater peer discipline.

5. PHYSICAL RESOURCES. Most of the innovative schools have new buildings and facilities that are designed to serve the educational programs. They provide the climate to facilitate the learning activities of students and the work of the staff. Others have relatively new buildings with additions and some major renovations. There are irreducible qualities of buildings and other facilities among the essential components of the educational environment that characterize these schools.

6. SCHOOL AND COMMUNITY RELATIONS. These schools open the curricula to an increasing number of adults to continue their education. Parents and other citizens participate as aides, consultants, research assistants, and in other roles.

A few schools are now at about 1976 on a 1980 timetable of development. Probably not over two-thirds of the secondary schools of America will reach this stage of development earlier than 1980, assuming favorable conditions for advancement. The other third may not arrive until 1990 unless the fundamental needs for their performance are provided soon.

Venn (1964) called attention to the rapidly declining opportunities for unskilled youth in the labor market. These young people, most often early school leavers but also including recent high school graduates, represent the segment of our population with the highest rate of unemployment — as high as 60 percent in some urban areas. Venn concluded that in view of rapid population increase this situation can be expected to deteriorate in the next five years when almost twice as many young people will enter the world of work with little if any occupational training. Entry jobs will not increase in this same period. The unemployed will continue to be the undereducated and underskilled, and no foreseeable rate of national growth can solve this employment problem. Universal occupational education from the elementary school through higher education for a substantial portion of the population was seen by Venn as the only solution to this pressing social problem. In his survey of schools he found little in the present school scene to suggest any major changes in this direction.[6]

Florida has been a perennial pioneer in the development and implementation of new programs in education. For example, the trend for many years has been to cram more and more into the elementary curriculum. Yet in many schools there is still something important lacking.

Few would dispute the need for education in the sciences and the humanities, but acceptance of the fact that technology is a dominant force in modern life (and should, therefore, be a part of the education of all) has been, in the face of other demands, slow in coming. Now, activity experiences related to technology and the world of work are becoming more and more a part of the K-6 scene through the medium of elementary school industrial arts.

Elementary industrial arts programs are underway in Lee, Broward, Alachua, Leon, and Brevard Counties in the state of Florida. Some of these programs are in the first, tentative, try-out phases. Others are full-blown programs backed by funding and in-service courses. The proposed state accreditation standards contain, for the first time, a section concerning elementary school industrial arts. Elsewhere in the country, programs of note are being conducted in California, North Carolina, Ohio, New York, Illinois (Chicago), Georgia, and many other states. In New Jersey, the well-known Technology for Children Project is now in its fourth year, under the guidance of a special section of the State Department of Education. New Jersey has long been a leader, with "manual training" in Montclair elementary schools as early as 1882.[7]

In 1969-70, 45 percent of all high school students were enrolled in vocational education. This compares to 37 percent in 1967-68. In 1974-75 an estimated 55 percent were enrolled in career education programs. The largest enrollment in Florida schools in 1970 was in Home Economics Education, 118,508 pupils. This was followed by Trades and Industrial Education, 25,942; Agriculture, 19,826; Office Occupations, 8,141; Work Experience Programs, 4,732;

Distributive Education, 4,163; Diversified Cooperative Training, 3,706; Technical Education, 839; and Health-Related Occupations, 599.[8]

The writer can vision this new secondary structure he has proposed as a design which should provide students with an upgraded type of instruction. The focal point of this change would be to assist teachers, parents and administrators to develop and acquire an attitude of change — an attitude correlated very closely to innovation, experimental work, working in joint-action with students and parents. We have enough adequate research at the moment, which if understood and applied to the classroom, could result in a renaissance which would retard our trip to the brink of chaos. We cannot afford to drift with little sense of direction. We should be thinking in terms of the following:

1. That education is really a "function of the federal government." We can no longer accept the premise that "education is a function of the state."
2. That education programs on the secondary level should begin pointing toward three goals, namely: a) realistic programs (for the parent); b) relevant programs (for the student) and c) educational programs which relate closely to socio-economic issues of society.
3. That the foundation for ALL learning is READING. We need an urgent and rational program for all American youth which will permit them the opportunity to read well enough to not only secure and retain a job, but to be able to accelerate to higher career positions throughout the working years.
4. That every high school youth should be the recipient of secondary school training which will provide them with a salable and marketable set of skills which business and industry might employ.
5. That teachers be trained in the techniques of measurement evaluation. The evaluation concept, now in use in our secondary schools, is archaic and obsolete. From one-third to one-half of the teachers in this country at the secondary school level are giving eroneous grades to high school students due to lack of training in measurement and evaluation. Institutions of higher education preparing candidates for teaching must offer better instruction in the area of evaluation. In-service

training programs staffed with adequately trained personnel is also needed.

6. That the American secondary school needs to set standards for youth to achieve. Clear standards exist in our system today: Little, if any, *sequence* and *articulation* of subject matter is apparent.

7. That the position of superintendent of schools and other central office staff be abolished in favor of a joint council of working principals. This model is now working in the Seattle Community College District where the three college presidents sit as co-equals as the executive under a board of trustees. County superintendents of schools can provide many functions now assumed by local school systems, including mass purchasing which can save on supply costs in addition to the savings effected by the reduction of administrative personnel at the local level.

8. That since NO subject at the high school level is more important than any other subject, the local board of education should abandon any set of subjects required for graduation. The student should be able to elect those things he or she deems most important. This means working more closely with the personnel associated with the guidance and counseling program.

9. That secondary school should stress the importance of being able to speak, write, listen, compute, think and understand. Subject matter should be integrated (for example, combining English and social studies) rather than taught as fragmentary items.

If the author's proposal for re-structuring of the high school is followed, there are several implications which follow:

A. Since students will be graduating at the age of about 14, our child labor laws will have to undergo some modification to permit the graduate the opportunity to market the skills he acquired in high school. The typical high school student of 14 is much more mature socially, physically, morally, emotionally and mentally than his counterpart of World War II.

B. The Bureau of Census (1970) has indicated that the median years of school completed by the white race between the ages of 20-44 is estimated to be 12.6 and for the Negro approximately 12.2 years of schooling. Utilizing the writer's proposals of requiring a "free" universal education which includes two years of college (the community college), we may state that most American youth's educational attainment should rise by an additional two years by the year 2000.

C. If increased educational attainment is realized over the next quarter century, we may see: (1) public welfare rolls decreased; (2) employment on the increase because of technological and scientific positions being available to utilize this higher mental maturity level of our expanding population and (3) the annual per capita income to increase significantly thus increasing the gross national income of this country.

D. Utilizing the proposed structure of the secondary school, no additional high schools would have to be constructed for the next 50 years. Why? For the simple reason that the last two years of the elementary school (grades 7 and 8) would comprise the first two years of high school and the current first two years of the secondary school (grades 9 and 10) would mark the last two years of our proposed high school. At the beginning of the school year 1969, there were 1,835,626 instruction rooms in the nation's public schools; 69,700 new ones had been completed and 18,315 had been abandoned in 1968-69, making a total gain of 51,385 rooms. WE HAVE A SUFFICIENT NUMBER OF ROOMS AVAILABLE to EDUCATE AMERICAN YOUTH — THERE IS NO NEED TO BUILD ANY MORE!

E. Assuming that this country might consider the construction of some 3000 elementary and 500 secondary schools within the next 25-year span, using the writer's restructuring plan would save the U.S. taxpayers an estimated $30 billion dollars.

---

[1]Jones, R. Stewart, "Instructional Problems and Issues," *Review of Educational Research*, Vol. XXXVI, No. 4, October 1966, p. 417.

[2]Less Time, More Options, Education Beyond The High School, A Special Report and Recommendations by *The Carnegie Commission on Higher Education*, New York: McGraw-Hill Book Company, January, 1971, p. 8.

3Blanchard, B. Everard. *A National Survey: Curriculum Articulation between the College of Liberal Arts and the Secondary School*, Second Interim Report, Graduate Programs Office, School of Education, De Paul University, Chicago, Illinois, Spring Quarter, 1971, p. 32.

4Blanchard, B. Everard. *A Comparative Analysis of Primary, Intermediate, Secondary, College and University Levels of Aptitude Versus Achievement*, Third Interm Report, Graduate Programs Office, School of Education, De Paul University, Chicago, Illinois, Winter Quarter, 1971, p. 10.

5McLure, William P., and Pence, Audra May. *Early Childhood and Basic Elementary and Secondary Education: Programs, Demands, Costs*. National Educational Finance Project. Special Study No. 1. Bureau of Educational Research, College of Education, University of Illinois at Urbana-Champaign, 1970, pp. 74-76.

6Jones, R. Stewart, "Instructional Problems and Issues," *Review of Educational Research*, Vol. XXXVI, No. 4, October 1966, p. 414.

7Resser, Arthur J., and John J. Geil, "New Look Counts Industrial Arts In," FLORIDA SCHOOLS (an official publication of the Department of Education, through the Public Information Services, Tallahasee, Florida) January-February 1970, pp. 29-31.

8Wade, Mitchell, "Florida School Facts," FLORIDA SCHOOLS, Bureau of Research, Department of Education, January-February 1971, p. 33.

❖ CHAPTER 7
Higher Education

TOTAL enrollments in higher education have reached an all time high though now leveling off somewhat. The U.S. college population, in fact, is estimated to be three times as large as that in all of Western Europe combined. For example, Figure 7-1 portrays these comparative enrollment figures between the number of college students of Western Europe versus students in the United States. It is estimated that approximately 8.4 million college

FIGURE 7-1
Western Europe vs. United States*

Country	Number of College Students	Students Per 1,000 Population
United States....................	7,920,000....................	39
Sweden	115,000....................	14
France..........................	684,000....................	13
Italy	556,000....................	10
Netherlands	106,000....................	8
England	459,000....................	8
Switzerland	42,000....................	7
Belgium........................	51,000....................	5
Austria	40,000....................	5
West Germany....................	306,000....................	5

*For the 1970-71 academic year.
Latest available figures from official agencies.

students are now enrolled in higher education in the United States, an increase of roughly 40 per cent in the past five-year period. Figure 7-2 indicates these results:

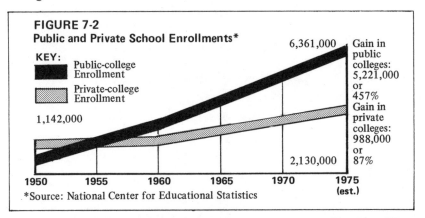

FIGURE 7-2
Public and Private School Enrollments*

KEY:
■ Public-college Enrollment
▓ Private-college Enrollment

6,361,000 — Gain in public colleges: 5,221,000 or 457%

1,142,000

Gain in private colleges: 988,000 or 87%

2,130,000

1950   1955   1960   1965   1970   1975 (est.)
*Source: National Center for Educational Statistics

By 1980, enrollment is expected to increase to about 10 million with 8 million in public and only 2 million in private institutions.

A factor which could alter future projections of college enrollments is centered in the rising costs of tuitions and fees which is becoming extremely difficult for the typical student. In some prestige colleges at the moment, tuition, board and room range from $15,000 to $20,000 for four years of undergraduate study. Figure 7-3 illustrates the costs of a college education:

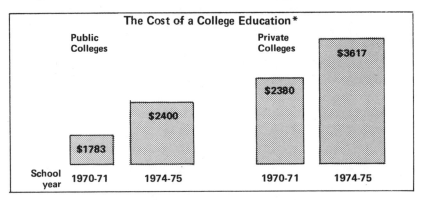

The Cost of a College Education*

Public Colleges   Private Colleges

$3617

$2380

$2400

$1783

School year   1970-71   1974-75   1970-71   1974-75

*Average charges for tuition, fees, room and board for full-time undergraduates. Costs at many colleges run much higher than the averages. Expenses of books, clothing, transportation and other items increase total outlays even higher. These figures represent tuition for State or local residents; out-of-state residents pay more than indicated. Source: College Scholarship Service.

In view of the January 1971 report and recommendations of *The Carnegie Commission on Higher Education*, Benjamin S. Bloom's *Stability and Change in Human Characteristics* and the writer's *A National Survey: Curriculum Articulation between the College of Liberal Arts and the Secondary School* an entirely new structure in higher education is hereby suggested. This proposal should have been implemented years ago. We are currently operating a chain of colleges and universities throughout the country on a "horse and buggy" basis while administrative officials of these same institutions drive around in air-conditioned, four-wheel disc brake and automatic transmission cars costing the taxpayers thousands of dollars. Some school officials even use airlines to cavort about the country on amusement as well as educational ventures of little value. Some Presidents even have the audacity to have homes built for their own personal use without even securing the approval of the governing bodies of these institutions of higher education. The writer is of the opinion: that in the beginning, geniuses may have invented colleges and universities, but currently, some of them are being run by idiots!

Three factors guide the formation of the NEW UNIVERSITY, namely: (1) We need to decrease the time necessary to acquire a complete and thorough education; (2) We need to provide the candidate in education more options of choice and (3) Emphasis upon technological, scientific and professional opportunities should be provided so that EVERYONE upon satisfactory completion of his or her education possesses a marketable skill for the business and industrial areas, whether the individual may seek employment, or desires to set up his own business.

The proposed structure of the new university advocated by the writer is indicated in Figure 7-4.

In reviewing Figure 7-4, five divisions of education are suggested, namely:

1. Grade levels 11 and 12 would comprise the community college. A student would study for a two-year period in some technological, scientific, or pre-professional area. Upon satisfactory completion of the work, the student could be granted either an Associate Certificate, or Associate Degree. This level of education would become an integral part of the *universal compulsory free education* offered to all American youth.

A New System of Education

FIGURE 7-4
The Proposed Structure of the University

Conventional:		Proposed:		Remarks:
Entrance Age: Estimated	Grade Level	Entrance Age: Estimated	Grade Level	For Proposed New Structure
18	13	15	11	First two years may be spent in technological, scientific, or pre-professional studies. An Associate Certificate, or Associate Degree may be conferred upon satisfactory completion.
19	14	16	12	
20	15	17	13	Three years of work may lead to the bachelor's degree. For example, a teacher would have three years of professional and specialized training, rather than two as currently provided.
21	16	18	14	Upon satisfactory completion of four years of academic training, the master's degree would be granted. Under this plan, a prospective teacher would have TWICE the amount of academic training (professional and specialized work) than her contemporary training provides.
22-23	17-18	19	15	The doctorate in education would be reduced to one year consisting of 12 months of work. A concentrated program comparable to the existing accelerated summer session would prevail. For some, the doctorate might be a prolonged affair; for others, it could be brief, intensive, yet mentally challenging.
23 and above		19 and above		Adult Education, or Continuing Education for those members of society who might be interested.

Addressing the Junior and Community Consortium of the Regional Education Laboratory of the Carolinas and Virginia, B. Lamar Johnson stated:[1] "The future of the American junior college, the most dynamic unit in American education, is inextricably interwoven with excellence in teaching. High quality teaching, in fact, will resolve most of the other challenges which the junior college is called upon to meet." Dr. Johnson cited eight new developments in junior college instruction which he said "represent promising departures from the lock-step of American education — and certainly from the stereotyped tradition of the lecture or lecture-discussion method."

Dr. Johnson listed the increased use of scientific instructional objectives, the "systems approach," programmed instruction, technological audio-visual aids, special facilities for large group instruction, students serving as teachers and tutors, sensitivity training and encounter groups, and cooperative work-study programs which relate classroom work to career interests and provide an income which often makes college attendance possible.

2. Grade 13 characterizes the three-year baccalaureate. Prospective candidates for teaching would acquire three years of specialized and professional work rather than the current two-year plan in vogue which has undoubtedly contributed to the inadequate training rendered to school personnel. And, this bachelor's degree could be earned at the age of 17, rather than the traditional age of 21. This four-year difference might represent a total financial savings of approximately $10,000 to $20,000 depending upon the school attended and the distance from the student's home.

3. Grade 14 represents the third phase of the proposed structure. A candidate having been granted the bachelor's degree in three years might decide to remain a fourth year and take the master's degree. Theoretically, a candidate for teaching taking the fourth year would have TWICE the amount of professional and specialized training prospective teachers currently secure. Procedure would certainly upgrade the teaching status of school personnel. And, on top of this, the work achieved by the candidates in education could be of high quality. The pursuit of a master's degree in education should not be characterized as GRADUATE work, but as certain levels of skills and competencies necessary to do the job as efficiently as possible. Additional work above and beyond the baccalaureate *should* be thought of as *professional* study, not as graduate level work for the simple reason that NO scientific study date has specifically claimed to be able to differentiate between undergraduate and graduate study.

4. The fourth phase begins at the grade 15 level; this is illustrated as work beyond the master's degree. In lieu of granting doctoral degrees, the writer would rather discard these ill-named documents and issue certificates, or diplomas as the grade school does. The ONLY doctoral degrees to be continued should be those in the fields of medicine, dentistry,

etc. WE SHOULD NOT CONFUSE THE PROFESSIONAL (doctor of medicine) with the NON-PROFESSIONAL (academic teacher). Doctoral degrees in the academic disciplines are quite misleading. In short, an academic degree, no matter what kind, is NO GUARANTEE OF COMPETENCE — IT NEVER HAS BEEN. And, it never will be!

5. The fifth phase of this newly structured educational program would focus its attention on the administration of Adult Education, or Continuing Education. Any American citizen interested in improving his cultural, socio-economic status, educational or occupational position might be a logical participant in this program. *No prescribed admission requirements would be necessary — the only real prerequisite would be — the individual's personal felt need and interest in improving himself or herself.*

The Need to Build More Colleges

The *Carnegie Commission on Higher Education* in forecasting future college enrollment figures states:[2] More than 16 million students will be enrolled in the nation's colleges and universities in 30 years. To accommodate these students, the country will need between 175 and 235 new community colleges and 80 to 105 more four-year colleges.

According to the *Illinois State Board of Higher Education*, no new four-year colleges should be built. Instead, the state should:

1. Better utilize existing colleges;
2. Improve admission procedures;
3. Direct more students to junior colleges or the job force, and
4. Find new methods — such as on-the-job training — to give more individuals an education.

Assuming that we were to follow the recommendations of the *Carnegie Commission on Higher Education* to build more Community colleges as well as four-year colleges, let us assume that within the next thirty years, we might build 400 of the institutions just cited. U.S. taxpayers would be faced with paying a debt estimated at between $25 to $50 billions of dollars! Using the author's new structure of education with the last two years of high school being the first two years of a college, or university, we would not have to build these institutions as advocated by the Carnegie Commission for the simple reason that they already exist! We could thus save Mr. John Q. public the billions of dollars just cited.

Since we have roughly 25,000 secondary schools throughout the United States, potentially we have a comparable number of Community colleges just waiting to serve the American citizens of this country. And, since we have an over-supply of teaching personnel available at the present, we would face NO serious problem in locating qualified teachers to staff these Community colleges. In the long haul of administering the nation's educational programs, it would be much easier to use existing buildings plus available teachers, than it would be to build entirely new buildings.

The Financial Status of Education[3]

The United States must adopt an entirely new concept to support the financial needs of the American educational system. The spiraling cost of education is a factor in the fiscal crisis facing government at every level. For example, in Pennsylvania, $1.7 billion or 56.3 percent of the annual state budget goes for education.

Schools in Philadelphia, Pittsburgh and in other cities of the commonwealth have been forced to reduce educational programs at many levels — kindergarten, special studies, interscholastic sports and music. Entire school districts in Ohio have been closed for lack of funds. Taxpayers all over the country have begun to organize against increasing property taxes for education.

The basic reason our cities and school districts are going broke is that we are trying to finance long-term investments out of current operating revenues. Even AT & T would go broke trying to do that.

A remedy is suggested — the creation of a National Education Trust Fund. The heart of this proposal is that education is an investment in the future growth of our people and of this nation, not a "cost of operation" for state or local government.

In operation, the fund might finance the crucial preschool years on a 90 percent Federal and 10 percent state and local fund basis — as we do for the principal interstate highways.

The trust fund might finance elementary and secondary school years on a 50-50 ratio and college and professional training on a 60-40 basis, or some other arrangement based upon more detailed

economic studies. The percentages are flexible, but the principle is
clear. We can use such a fund to give emphasis where needed.

Control of the schools, of course, would remain with the local
communities. And, with the Federal Government assuming an
increasing role in the funding of education, state and local
educational burdens could be reduced. Also, we could expect large
reductions in the welfare and other social-service costs which stem
from the inability of uneducated and untrained persons to
participate meaningfully in our society.

Every dollar we invest in the education of a young person is
repaid many times over during his lifetime from the taxes he pays.
Moreover, statistics show that the better his education, the more
money he can earn; consequently, the more taxes he pays.

The G.I. Bill of Rights from World War II is a clear example of
the economic returns that can be expected from Federal investment
in education. The Government invested $19 billion in this effort,
and by 1968, over $64 billion in increased taxes had been collected
directly from the recipients of the program.

There is no other investment that can be made in the public
sector of our economy that will provide as direct and measurably
higher yield. More and higher quality education leads to greater
productivity. Greater productivity leads to higher personal and
corporate earning power.

Conversely, the failure to invest adequately in education is
costing this nation dearly. The rising crime rate and welfare rolls
are indicators of this failure. For every dollar we have failed
to invest in adequate education we are now paying many times
over in increased funds for police protection, prisons and public
assistance.

We can create a large-scale revolving fund by requiring those
who would benefit most through increased educational opportunities to repay the fund with a small continuing surtax after
they became wage earners.

This parallels the plan whereby relatively low Federal taxes levied
on gasoline and certain auto supplies paid by the users of the
highways replenish the highway trust fund and pay for the
construction of new roads.

It is obvious that we would not have our modern, interstate
highway system if we had left the task of financing new roads to our
states, cities and townships alone. Yet, this is precisely what we are

doing with our present fragmented system for financing education throughout the country.

None of the individual aspects of establishing such an education fund are revolutionary. The concept is similar to the highway trust fund. The surcharge on Federal income taxes is not unlike that levied to finance the Vietnam war. The free education and deferred payment plan is similar to existing scholarship and loan programs and to deferred tuition plans.

Parents do not view their children as a "cost item" but as an investment in the future. It's time that Government embraced this reality and instituted the concept of investment in education.

In the Report of the Resolutions Committee of the *American Association For Higher Education*, it is cited:[4]

> We recognize that in the allocation of resources, increased funds spent on educational programs will require changes in national priorities and in the sources of funds. However, we believe that federal aid to education supports those activities essential to the solution of major national problems and without the contribution of education those problems will not be solved.

The following recommendations are not meant to minimize the significant responsibility of the states for their support of higher education. We recommend that the federal government should:

1. recognize that the national interest is served by placing a high priority on education and acknowledge the vital contribution of education to all major national objectives. Short run efforts to control national expenditures should not sacrifice our basic investment in the education and future productivity of American youth.
2. greatly increase its support for educational research and innovation and guarantee long-term support for those educational programs that are found to be effective.
3. enact educational appropriations before the beginning of the fiscal year and make program funds available to schools and colleges before the beginning of the academic year.
4. authorize multiyear commitments to educational programs and projects.
5. provide higher levels of support for Educational Opportunity Grants, National Defense Student Loans, and work-study

programs and fund in advance all of these programs on the same calendar basis.

6. provide increased federal support for all higher education facilities programs.

7. commit itself to establish a new long-term program of general institutional support for public and private institutions. Such a program should encourage a free flow of students across the borders.

8. provide adequate funds to insure the survival and improve the quality of the predominantly black institutions without decreasing its commitment to full integration of faculties and student bodies in all institutions of higher education.

9. insure the availability of both old and new forms of communications media and technology for educational and public service purposes.

Innovative Institutions of Higher Education

A new commission is being formed at De Pauw University with the view of restructuring the academic program so that it will be in accord with higher education's changing needs. It will include faculty, administrators, trustees and students.

Dr. William E. Kerstetter, De Pauw University President cited the following as examples of new educational aims that are to be examined:[5]

1. Shortening of the time (and reducing student costs) required for a student to get from high school thru college and his vocation or profession.

2. Perhaps condensing or coordinating liberal arts education more perfectly with such professions as medicine, engineering and law to shorten the period of formal education.

3. Obtaining greater productivity from the functions of the instructional process.

A Report to the Commission on the Future of the College from Marvin Bressler for Discussion by the Princeton University Community is indeed enlightening:[6]

Many observers, among them President Goheen, have noted that so many of our students seem to be bringing into freshman year higher levels of competence than used to be the case. [13] If catalogue descriptions of college preparatory courses (See Appendix II) are any index of what is actually learned then it is clear that the better public and private schools have already assumed responsibility for much of the general education that is now taught in freshman and sophomore college classes. By the end of the twelfth year, many students have been introduced to Sartre and Genet, Sophocles and Aristotle, to Marx and Freud, and routinely achieve a level of sophistication that would have been regarded as precocious for their parents. These impressions are corroborated by B. Everard Blanchard whose effort to assess the degree of overlap between high school and college curricula is the most recent and ambitious study of its kind. National samples of college and high school teachers cooperated in evaluating the extent of repetition in syllabi of courses in English, science, social studies and mathematics that are ordinarily taught both in grades eleven and twelve and the first two years of college. Blanchard concludes that "nearly one-third of the content of college teaching during the first two years represents a restoration of what has already been taught at the secondary level. [7] The mean percent of duplication in specific areas at the college level is for social science 39%, English 35%, science 24% and mathematics 22%. These findings are subject to the usual methodological caveats but they seem credible to many persons who are familiar with the progress of both colleges and secondary schools.

One of the major recommendations of the *Commission on the Future of the College* is:[8]

1. Princeton University should adopt a three-year undergraduate program with a limited option to pursue a fourth year of study.

It is indeed refreshing and certainly stimulating to know that such a distinguished and eminent institution as Princeton University is seriously considering the possibility of a three-year baccalaureate. And, possibly the fourth year granting the master's degree. This unique venture of Princeton University seems to coincide with the restructuring emphasis suggested by the author of this volume.

Northwestern University and Central YMCA Community College announced in 1971 the formation of an Urban Doctors Program to educate 25 physicians annually from Chicago's poverty neighborhoods. This program provides full tuition scholarships for two years of premedical education at Central Y, and four years of medical school at Northwestern. The cost will be from $30,000 to $35,000 per student.

John Daugirdas, a Northwestern medical student, stated that "Northwestern and Central Y are the first institutions to try it." Dr. Richard Kessler, director of the program, said the urban doctors would be expected to maintain the same standards in medical school as other students. Admission to Northwestern for all 25 students will be guaranteed upon successful completion of the Central Y two-year curriculum.[9]

A unique approach in changing the structure of the University is suggested by Dr. Walter Perry, Vice Chancellor of Open University as he states:[10] Entry is open to anyone whether or not he has academic qualifications. Our degree will be good. It has to be. Anything different will not be worth the paper it was written on.

What Open University seeks to do is enable students to study and earn academic degrees in three to five years while working at their jobs. The students range from coal miners to professional football players to ministers. Nearly 25,000 students seeking degrees began taking courses January 1, 1971 in Open University, an experiment that blends television and radio lectures, home studies, monthly correspondence packets, meetings with tutors at local study centers and a week of summer school. The University goes far beyond correspondence schools in the United States in its use of summer schools.

Following a year-long study by the faculty, students and administrative staff, Chatham College has adopted a new academic program which frees the student from traditional requirements and gives her an opportunity to design the course of study which best fulfills her personal educational interests and abilities. Such an approach is possible only in a college like Chatham.

Under the New Curriculum at Chatham, the requirement for graduation is the satisfactory completion of a choice of 34 courses, including two interim programs and a tutorial. The interim programs will provide month-long, differently structured and especially intensive work in a field of special student interest. The senior tutorial — an individual study project designed by the student and a faculty advisor, and requiring competent oral and written articulation — will now be the only formal academic experience common to all Chatham students. The underlying assumption of the New Curriculum is that students and faculty members are participating scholars. The New Calendar provides them with an open, manageable timetable in which to share and individually pursue their academic concerns. Each student will determine which method of grading will be most useful and appropriate to her work.[11]

The Faculty at Bowdoin College has voted to eliminate the College Board examination requirement for admission candidates. Effective with applicants for the Class of 1974, the submission of CEEB-SAT and Achievement Test scores to the College is optional.[12]

An undergraduate editorial in the Brown University *Daily Herald* says it well: "The changing nature of education . . . and the increasing involvement of students in socio-political movements makes it essential now that the entire range of admissions be reexamined . . . The challenges of the new curriculum and the proposed modification in the overall atmosphere of intellectual life . . . bring into focus the importance of attracting and accepting a highly creative, highly motivated class of students." And Eugene Wilson, Dean of Admissions at Amherst College, brings the point into closer focus by discussing tests: "Aptitude Test scores at their best predict marks and are validated by marks; but neither marks nor test scores are reliable indicators of the ability to think or reason. Test scores do not guarantee the presence of those human qualities and intellectual abilities we value most."

It has often been assumed that College Board scores correlate well with performance patterns in college. Recent studies at Bowdoin College have prompted us to question this assumption.

Evaluation in Higher Education

St. Louis University located in St. Louis, Missouri is the foremost Catholic institution of higher education in the nation today. With its curricular offerings in Business, Chemistry, Engineering (civil, electrical, geological, geophysical, industrial), Hospital Administration, Law, Medical Record Librarian, Medical Technology, Medicine, Nursing, Physical Therapy, Psychology, Social Work, Teacher Education and Theology, and with slightly more than 10,000 enrollees engaged in the various programs, the President of the University, The Very Reverend Paul C. Reinert, S.J., provides an educational leadership which is impeccable and without a parallel in Catholic higher education.

For example, writing in an educational journal, President Reinert mentioned that St. Louis University has taken 10 steps to implement academic planning. These steps are ennumerated as follows:

1. *Determine target year.* The target year should not be too near nor too far away. Ten years is too long. Five years is about right.

2. *Set up general parameters.* These should be as accurate as possible predictions of key factors influencing curricular offerings and research. Examples would include estimates of student-credit hour production and full-time equivalent positions in departmental budgets.

3. *Have each planning unit* (such as a department or division) develop a "role and scope" summing up the department's hopes for the target year in terms of enrollment, course offerings, faculty size, research and public service programs. In other words, what will the department look like in the target year?

4. *Bring together key planners* to discuss role and scope and explain the general parameters. Key planners include the dean, departmental chairman, selected faculty, graduate dean where applicable, and coordinator of planning.

5. *Have departmental chairman* and selected faculty develop revised role and scope statement plus specific picture of target year enrollments by class, needed faculty and staff personnel, and source of revenues for specific research contemplated.

6. *Bring all key planners together* again to go over plan, check aspirations against realistic general parameters, and approve departmental plan as final.

7. *Focus departmental plans into one over-all plan* for the next highest organizational unit, such as division, school or college.
8. *Determine priority needs* in light of plans of all departments. Determine departments to be significantly developed, those to be maintained at current levels, those to be developed later rather than in the current planning period, and those to be discontinued.
9. *Summarize each departmental plan* and the general plan for feedback from groups to be consulted, such as all full-time faculty of the college.
10. *Plan to update all plans annually* by moving target date year up one, and adjusting predictions and plans on the basis of additional year's experience. [13]

Another interesting viewpoint is expressed by W. Robert Houston in speaking of Michigan State University and its *Behavioral Science Elementary Teacher Education Program* as related to the evaluation component:[14] A viable teacher education program requires a carefully designed, extensive and workable evaluation system which in turn supports program development. Cognitive, affective, and psychomotor domains must be included in such assessments. In the past, evaluations have been hampered by lack of information vis-a-vis the student and teacher personal characteristics, specific program components, and the social milieu in which the teacher is functioning. In a sense, evaluation permeates the entire program. It is a necessary and fundamental aspect of the clinical style; it forms the basis for program modification and development; and it is inherent in instructional strategies. While the model report describes the evaluation system in some detail, this summary is limited to one facilitating phase — an information retrieval system.

Syracuse University states its concept of the evaluation component as follows:[15] Evaluation procedures are the responsibility of the information and evaluation support system. It is these procedures which provide the information on which program modification and refinement are based. In addition, the system is charged with the task of gathering information about student progress and feeding this information back to the student and the instructional staff in a form which is useful in facilitating the student's self-paced progress through the program. The evaluation system is also used in assessing the effectiveness of the program (process) for students with different characteristics (presage) in terms of the program's ability to foster the development of competent, self-directed, self-renewing teachers (product). Finally, it is a function of this system to disseminate findings derived from a study of the experimental program to other teacher education institutions.

The evaluation of the ongoing program is seen as process evaluation focusing on the use of formative data as feedback into the system. The evaluation of student progress implies a monitoring function. An evaluation strategy that requires process, presage, and product measures is suggested by the need to examine program outputs in terms of program inputs and throughouts. The dissemination function depends upon the careful explication which only carefully conducted research and evaluation can provide.

It must be remembered that the self-renewing aspect of the program is largely dependent upon the adequacy of the evaluation process.

Teachers College, Columbia University views evaluation as:[16] The evaluation of achievement is embedded in the methods as they have been described. Each feedback group monitors its members progress through the mastery of the maneuvers, the models, the development of models within the curriculum areas, and the creation of original teaching strategies. Because the creation and implementation of original teaching strategies is conducted as an experiment, the evaluation procedures have to be constructed in order to carry out the activities.

It should be stressed that achievement of the objectives of this subcomponent is essential to the success of the teacher education program. Only a very narrow tolerance of underachievement can be made. A student who does not develop the basic repertoire of teaching maneuvers and strategies will be an educational cripple.

The University of Toledo takes this attitude toward the evaluation concept:[17] The term, "evaluation," is used in two ways in the teacher education model. One component of each specification is entitled "evaluation." This component deals specifically with procedures or materials necessary for evaluating whether the behavioral objectives of that specification have been met. This is a very specific use of evaluation, and in implementing the specifications, a teacher would be utilizing large numbers of these evaluation components. Such components are specific to the instructional task of implementing the specifications."

Evaluation is also used as a more general concept which applies continuous feedback and decisionmaking throughout the implementation of the model. In this context the purpose of evaluation is to provide information for decisionmaking, and in order to evaluate, it is therefore necessary to know the decisions to be served. For this purpose, the evaluation design must meet the criteria of validity, reliability, and objectivity. The general evaluation designed for this model follows a single set of generalizable steps which will enable the decisionmaker to make decisions throughout the implementation of the model. Thus, evaluation is an ongoing and continuous process concurrent with implementation.

There is little disagreement among educators as to the direction that should be taken in developing evaluative methods and instruments of measurement. Evaluation should be made for the purpose of helping children, youth, and adults, through their own efforts, to become better individuals and to improve their conditions of living. It is to the kind and extent of these changes that evaluation must be directed. In the past, it has been much more common practice to measure some intangible aspect of the educational program such as specific information learned by the pupils or the teacher's methods and materials of instruction, assuming that the factor measured had a positive correlation with the purpose of the school, and to form judgment on this basis. The most serious difficulty in this procedure has been that the indicative aspects of the school which are thus measured tend to become ends in themselves; ardently sought by teachers, pupils, and administrators, while the real purposes of the school are neglected.[18]

Questionable Admission Practices

If one reviews the various college catalogs regarding the admission practices of institutions of higher education, one may see a very traditional image prevailing. That is, we may find many colleges and universities requiring the Scholastic Aptitude Test (SAT), the American College Testing Program (ACT), the College Entrance Examination Board (CEEB), or possibly, the college has devised its own testing program if the student does not submit scores on either SAT or ACT.

According to research, it appears that requiring such testing for entrance into an institution of higher education may be "much adieu about nothing."

A *Ford Foundation* study at Brown University reveals that students classified as "admission risks" go on to perform just as well as their better qualified classmates. In investigating the further careers of 2100 "risks" over a seven-year period, researchers came to the following conclusions:[19]

1) Risk students complete their undergraduate courses almost as often as high college board scorers.
2) Although a bit less likely to be admitted to graduate school, they do as well there as other students.
3) Risks are just as likely to achieve career success as other students.

The Brown University report concludes that the traditional criteria of college admissions — college board scores and high school grades — do not present the whole picture. Equally important is the factor of motivation.

One implication of this study is that traditional admissions requirements can be lowered without seriously affecting academic standards, despite what critics of open admissions have charged.

The faculty of Bowdoin College has voted to eliminate the College Board examination requirement for admission candidates. Beginning with applicants to the Class of 1974, the submission of CEEB-SAT and Achievement Test scores to the College became optional.[20]

Of the Bowdoin students who graduated Cum Laude, Magna Cum Laude, Magna Cum Laude or Summa Cum Laude in the Classes of 1968 and 1969, only 31% had entered the College with both SAT's above their class medians, while 24% had entered the College with both SAT's below their class medians. (The incoming class medians were V-605, M-658 for '68, and V-610, M-650 for '69.) In both of these classes, averaging 250 men, at least one student graduated with Latin Honors whose SAT's were both below 500. In the Class of 1969, one man graduated Cum Laude who had entered Bowdoin with a Verbal of 475 and a Math of 386.

In an Admissions Office poll of the Bowdoin faculty, professors were asked to list the names of recent students who were the best representatives of the qualities Bowdoin should be most eager to attract, and also " . . . those students you have taught during the last few years who are models of what Bowdoin could do without." In profiling both groups as they had entered Bowdoin from secondary schools, statistics regarding College Board tests were particularly interesting: for example, 50 percent of the "models of what we can do without" had entered College scoring above their class medians on the SAT-V, and 65 percent of the same group entered Bowdoin scoring above their class median on the SAT-M.

"Correct Interpretation" is the key to maximum usefulness of standardized test scores in the evaluation of college candidates. However, uniformly correct interpretation by candidates and their families, school counselors, admissions officers and faculty committees, is almost too much to hope for. In many cases the scores can mislead, and the candidate would be better served by their absence from the admissions folder.

Our Maladjusted Entrance Requirements

The myopic prescription in college and university bulletins of certain subjects that must be completed as well as submitting scores on the Scholastic Aptitude Test (SAT) in order to be considered as a likely candidate for admission to an institution of higher education has been and continues to be *directly* contrary to the purposes and aims cited by many colleges and universities.

The determination of reasonable admission policies in higher education is a matter deserving special inquiry. Many surveys have suggested the need for a complete reorganization in this area. The system of higher education should be developed as an integral part of the system of public education similar to what the University of Michigan suggested in 1871 when it based its college admissions methods "on the theory that the university was a part of the public school system of the state."[21]

Colleges and universities should be pioneers, not mere *camp followers*. Their task is not limited to preserving and passing on a heritage of knowledge and treasured experience; they must take account of advancing knowledge, add to it when they can, sift and create as well as accumulate.

Some colleges and universities encourage all students to complete 16 high school academic units and then prescribe in writing the courses and units required. For example:

4 units in English
2 units in one foreign language
2 units in mathematics
1 unit in a laboratory science
1 unit in history

Hundreds of reputable research studies, almost without exception, have shown that the grades earned in universities and colleges have practically no relationship at all to what subjects were taken in high school. Students who have taken many units in a foreign language, English, mathematics, and science make no better grades in college than those who have done much less work in these fields but who have the same intelligence quotient or college aptitude test score. Some investigations show that abler students tend to do better work in mathematics, science, and foreign languages, particularly the last, and that, therefore, they make somewhat higher grades.[22]

While many institutions still cling to the old theory that good college students may be selected on the basis of subjects they have studied in high school, some colleges and universities have abandoned the practice. They content themselves with requiring the minimum of credit in the academic subjects, usually ten or eleven units after the eighth grade, which must include three units of English.[23]

Thirty selected secondary schools carried on an investigation of the post high school achievement of 1,475 students who were admitted to college regardless of the pattern of subjects taken in high school. The achievements of these students were compared to achievements of a control group made up of individuals who were selected to be equivalent, on the average, in intellectual capacity, age, and average school marks and who had taken the subjects prescribed for entrance to the college they attended. The ratio of males to females was the same in both groups. Cooperating colleges and universities agreed to accept the experimental students. In 1942, after eight years of study, the Commission on Relations Between High School and College, of the Progressive Education Association, reported that the experimental students:

(1) earned a slightly higher total grade average in college;
(2) earned higher grade averages in all subject fields except foreign languages;
(3) received slightly more academic honors each year;
(4) were more often judged to possess a high degree of intellectual curiosity and drive;
(5) were more often judged to be precise, systematic, and objective in their thinking;
(6) were more often judged to have developed clear or well-formulated ideas concerning the meaning of education, especially in the first two years of college;
(7) more often demonstrated a high degree of resourcefulness in meeting new situations;
(8) had about the same problem of adjustment as the comparison group, but approached their solution with greater effectiveness;
(9) participated somewhat more frequently, and more often enjoyed appreciative experiences, in the arts;
(10) participated more in all organized student groups except religious and "service" activities;
(11) earned in each college year a higher percentage of non-academic honors (officership in organizations, election to managerial activities, athletic insignia, leading roles in dramatic and musical activities);
(12) had a somewhat better orientation toward the choice of vocation, and
(13) demonstrated a more active concern for what was going on in the world.[24]

A follow-up investigation of the 55 students in the Eight-year Study who had graduated from the Ohio State University High School in 1938 and who were still alive and could be located, the following facts were revealed:

> These students were taught definitely on the basis of progressive education including core programs, pupil participation in planning, parent-teacher interviews, parent-teacher conferences, individualized reading programs and no report cards. In their school they were nourished on a strict diet of democratic living and working. More than 50 of the 55 are now successful

people, all of them are useful members of society. They can contribute to their communities at a higher level than others. Sixteen members of the class have publications, another had a novel in the hands of a publisher. They all read more than the national average; they all earn more than the national average. Thirty-four of the 55 graduated from college; 17 received one or more honors in college; 12 took master's degrees and 4 took doctor's degrees. Seventy-three percent entered the army as privates during World War II and only one remained at the rank at the time of discharge. Forty percent became commissioned officers and more than one-half of them became non-commissioned officers. Among those successful in business and political life there doesn't seem to be a single "Babbitt."[25]

The North Central Association of Colleges and Secondary Schools in 1962 made some nine recommendations of which three appear pertinent to this study, namely:

1) That colleges must accept greater responsibility for the success of the students whom they admit.

2) That more emphasis be placed by the colleges for admissions purposes upon the school's recommendations.

3) That college admissions policies be kept sufficiently flexible for the college to be able to admit members of groups whose low test scores are caused by deprived background or minority status.

The futility of requiring high school students to take the Scholastic Aptitude Test, (the Verbal and Mathematical portions plus the Achievement Tests) has long been demonstrated but the lethargic attitude of the educationists has become progressively worse.

Although it is clear from the correlations for V and M that the two parts are not measuring the same thing, it is also clear that whatever is being measured by one is also being measured by the other to a considerable extent. Correlations of .54 and .64 between measures of presumably different aptitudes are not a good sign. The overlap in variables is undesirably high.[26]

The achievement tests of SAT have about as much value as the aptitude tests. For example, the achievement coefficients show that scores from chemistry do not correlate appreciably higher with grades in chemistry than do scores from tests purporting to measure other things. As a matter of fact, the test which proved to be the best indicator of success in chemistry was biology. It is of more than incidental interest to note that scores from social studies, which correlate .50 with grades in chemistry, correlate .53 with grades in history and .53 with grades in political science.

Despite widespread use, there seems to be little evidence for believing that a particular achievement test of the CEEB measures specifically what it purports to measure. The available evidence indicates that the achievement tests are *not* good measures of proficiency in specific subjects.[27]

Available research results strongly suggest that the College Board examinations do *not* meet the minimum test standards commonly accepted by members of the testing fraternity.[28]

In view of the evidence cited, the author recommends that the typical college and university specific subject matter requirements for admission and the Scholastic Aptitude Test (SAT) be extended a permanent leave of absence. The following proposals for admission policies are tentatively suggested:[29]

1) Each college and university should organize a "Policies Committee," composed of members representing the varied academic disciplines, this committee to be directly responsible for gauging the admission of Freshmen students.
2) The "Policies Committee" should direct admission practices to be commensurate with the aims and objectives of the institution of higher education.
3) Each policy for admission of Freshmen students should be the result of cooperative joint action in regular session of the "Policies Committee." Each policy acceptable to this group

should be endorsed, approved, and adopted. These policies
should be spelled out in writing.

4) The CEEB tests should be eliminated as well as the specific
subject matter requirements.

5) The recommendations of the proper high school authorities
should be given much more weight than they are at the
present.

6) Secondary school authorities should furnish institutions of
higher education with a profile of the student's achievements,
not merely in the academic pursuits, but in the areas of
leadership, unusual talents, character, effort, industry, etc.

7) Institutions of higher education should furnish high schools
with profiles of their high school graduates. Lack of proper
articulation exists at present.

8) Colleges and universities should cooperate with secondary
schools to the extent of constructing and developing desirable
entrance requirements which will take into account groups of
students who may be classified as culturally deprived or
coming from minority groups.

Implications for Collegiate Planning

Alexander W. Astin has completed a carefully controlled research
project using some 38 institutions, most of them liberal arts
colleges. His findings seem to suggest several implications for
planning, namely:[30]

1) It may be wise to re-examine traditional notions about institutional excellence, particularly as it relates to the intellectual
development of students. The pursuit of brighter students,
more money, better libraries and physical plants, more
Ph.D.'s on the faculty, and other traditional indices of quality
will not necessarily produce a better environment for learning.

2) Another implication for planning concerns the general
question of admissions. Selective admissions policies cannot
necessarily be justified on the grounds that they create an
environment which is more conducive to student achievement.
Thus, institutions that wish to modify selective admissions
policies and diversify their student populations can do so
without the fear that the achievement of their brightest students will suffer as a consequence. By the same token, the

data suggest that the less able student will not necessarily wither and die when confronted by the overwhelming competition of a selective institution. The widely held belief that only the highly able student can profit from being exposed to the center of excellence is not confirmed. A different rationale for selective admissions has to be developed if the practice is to be continued without becoming cynical or hypocritical.

From the beginning, the great majority of colleges and universities have required for entrance specific subjects, particularly English, mathematics, foreign languages, and, in many cases, science and history. Hundreds of investigations have been made to check the validity of such criteria. Almost without exception, these studies have shown that the grades made in universities and colleges have practically NO relationship at all to what subjects were taken in high school. Students who have taken many units in a foreign language, English, mathematics, and science make no better grades in college than those who have done much less work in these fields but who have the same intelligence quotient or college-aptitude test score.[31]

The Eight-Year Study and A Follow-Up Twenty Years Later[32] have definitely cancelled the belief that the college-preparatory track offered in some secondary schools throughout the country is valid. No subject at the high school level is superior to any other subject. If this is true, WHY do colleges and universities persist in following such an antiquated idea?

Another archaic idea that medical schools throughout the country follow is that all students must have premedical work prior to being admitted to the medical school. Buehler and Trainer have stated:[33] "good premedical students are good medical students," but pointing out also that 20 percent of the poorer premedical students graduated in the top half of their respective classes and 10 percent of the better premedical students graduated in the bottom half.

Nonintellectual factors were also studied. Meile found personal adjustment of first-year law students to be independent of their grades, but he was able to conclude that the later a student decided to enter law, the harder it was for him to adjust to law school. This seems to contradict another generalizatin of his: the stronger a student's desire to become a lawyer, the higher his grades but the poorer his adjustment. Eichorn and Kallas found a significant relationship, using chi square, when they studied dropping out of engineering school and such factors as mother's education, siblings' education, financing from parents, and fraternity membership. Finally, Martin found success and failure in nursing school significantly related to scores on achievement and intelligence tests.[34]

It is the writer's opinion that requiring law students and medical students to have pre-law and pre-medical work is unnecessary. A candidate for teaching goes direct from high school to his teacher training program — general education and then his specialized and professional course training. Teaching is as complex and intricate as either law or medicine. *No scientific studies have ever substantiated the necessity for pre-law, or pre-med training as currently required.* It is time that someone take action to abandon these excess requirements which are wholly defenseless.

Inasmuch as the first two years of college are often wasted by the candidate attending college, the author would be most willing to abandon the requirement of a bachelor's degree in order to study medicine, or the requirement of a baccalaureate prior to being admitted to the law school. While these requirements may have been adequate some 40 to 50 years ago, the youngsters coming from our public and private schools of today have been exposed to a great deal more knowledge and opportunity than their predecessors of four or five decades past. Moreover, teachers today are much better prepared than their fellowmen of yesterday.

Benjamin S. Bloom has pointed out that by the age of four, a child has acquired about 50 percent of his mental maturity and by the age of eight, he has reached an estimated 80 percent of his mental maturity. At age eight, a child is generally in grade two of our conventional educational system. Since the child may have four more grades to complete in the six-year elementary school, would it be reasonable to assume that he has acquired another 10 percent of mental maturity? If we may assume that this is possible, and no one knows the maximum mental maturity level of any individual, suppose we add another 10 percent of mental maturity, this totals 100 percent. *And this student is just completing his elementary school education.* If we may further assume that these generalizations are correct, just *what does the high school and college accomplish with respect to an individual's mental maturity?*

There is no scientific evidence to indicate that either the secondary school or college attendance has anything to do with enhancing *brain power*. About all that can be said of a high school education, or a college or university education, is that the years spent by the individual sitting in a seat, taking notes, and coughing up on examination time what the instructor wants to hear may be merely postponing the opportunity to go to work, vis-a-vis, the memorization of facts is soon lost if not associated with the learner's needs.

As Robert Ingersol once said: Would that every man could go to college to see how little value there is in it.

To study for a profession as medicine, law, dentistry, or the ministry — there *is* a place in America for the college or university. To merely study for a degree is debatable.

---

[1]*Junior College Journal*, December/January, 1970, p. 48.

[2]Contact Verne Stadt, *Carnegie Commission on Higher Education*, 1947 Center Street, Berkeley, California 94704.

[3]Shapp, Milton J., "An Education Trust Fund," *The New York Times*, Saturday, October 30, 1971. Milton J. Shapp is Governor of the State of Pennsylvania.

[4]Report of the Resolutions Committee, *American Association For Higher Education*, 25th National Conference on Higher Education, The Conrad Hilton, Chicago, Illinois, March 1-4, 1970.

[5]Kerstetter, William E., President of De Pauw University, Greencastle, Indiana, "De Pauw University Eyes Need for Change," *The Chicago Tribune*, Thursday, May 13, 1971.

[6]*A Report to the Commission on the Future of the College from Marvin Bressler for Discussion by the Princeton University Community*, 58 Prospect Avenue — Elm Club, Princeton, New Jersey 08540, November 1971, p. 16. (The footnote 13 refers to Robert F. Goheen quoted in Bergen County *Record*, August 17, 1971).

[7]Refers to the author's national survey presented in Chapter 3 of this volume.

[8]*Op. Cit.*, p. 1.

[9]Nichol, Judy. "Tell plan to train urban area doctors," *The Chicago Sun-Times*, Tuesday, April 20, 1971, p. 3.

[10]*The Chicago Tribune*, "Open University Doors Open to All Britons," Thursday, May 13, 1971 (Bletchley, England).

[11]Personal communication with President Edward D. Eddy, Jr., Chatham College, Pittsburgh, Pennsylvania 15232.

[12]Personal communication with Dr. Richard W. Moll, Director of Admissions, Bowdoin College, Brunswick, Maine 04011.

[13]The Very Reverend Paul C. Reinert, S.J., President of St. Louis University, St. Louis, Missouri, "St. Louis University Takes a Systematic Approach," *College and University Business*, McGraw-Hill Publication, August 1969, p. 37.

[14]Houston, W. Robert, "A Guide to Behavioral Science Elementary Teacher Education Program," Michigan State University, *A Reader's Guide to the Comprehensive Models for Preparing Elementary Teachers*, ERIC Clearinghouse on Teacher Education and American Association of Colleges for Teacher Education, One Dupont Circle, Washington D.C./December 1969, p. 43.

[15]Weber, Wilford A., "A Guide to Specifications for a Comprehensive Undergraduate and Inservice Teacher Education Program for Elementary Teachers," Syracuse University, *A Reader's Guide to the Comprehensive Models for Preparing Elementary Teachers*, ERIC Clearinghouse on Teacher Education and American Association of Colleges for Teacher Education, One Dupont Circle, Washington, D.C./December 1969, p. 101.

[16]Joyce, Bruce R., "A Guide to The Teacher-Innovator: A Program to Prepare Teachers," Teachers College, Columbia University, *A Reader's Guide to the Comprehensive Models for Preparing Elementary Teachers*, ERIC Clearinghouse on Teacher Education and American Association of Colleges for Teacher Education, One DuPont Circle, Washington, D.C./December 1969, p. 153.

[17]Wiersma, William, "A Guide to Educational Specifications for a Comprehensive Elementary Teacher Education Program," The University of Toledo, *A Reader's Guide to the Comprehensive Models for Preparing Elementary Teachers*, ERIC Clearinghouse on Teacher Education and American Association of Colleges for Teacher Education, One Dupont Circle, Washington, D.E./December 1969, pp. 205-206.

[18]Blanchard, B. Everard, "The Meaning of Evaluation in Education," *Bulletin of the National Association of Secondary-School Principals*, May 1956, p. 44.

[19]*Parade*, "College Long Shots," November 29, 1970.

[20]Personal correspondence with the Director of Admissions, Dr. Richard W. Moll, Bowdoin College, Brunswick, Maine.

[21]Douglas, Harl R. *Secondary Education in the United States*. Second Edition. New York: The Ronald Press, 1964, p. 385.

[22]*Ibid.*, p. 388.

[23]*Ibid.*, pp. 388-389.

[24]Aiken, Wilford, M., *The Story of the Eight-year Study*. New York: Harper and Row, 1942, pp. 111-112.

[25]Willis, Margaret and Lou LaBrant, "The Guinea Pigs After Twenty Years: A Follow-Up Study of the Class of 1938 of the University School at Ohio State." Columbus: Ohio State University Press, 1962, pp. 32-36.

[26]*The Sixth Year Mental Measurements Yearbook*. Edited by Oscar K. Buros. Reprint of a review of the College Entrance Examination Board Admissions Testing Program by Benno G. Fricke. New Jersey: The Gryphon Press, Highlands Park, 1965, p. 978.

[27]*Ibid.*, p. 979.

[28]*Ibid.*, p. 979.

[29]Blanchard, B. Everard, "Our Maladjusted Entrance Requirements," *Improving College and University Teaching*, Volume XX, Number 3, Summer 1972, pp. 124-125.

[30]Astin, Alexander W., "New Research Has Implications For Academic Planning and the Quest for "Excellence", *College and University Business*, McGraw-Hill Publication, August 1969, p. 32.

[31]Douglass, Harl R. *Secondary Education in the United States*. Second Edition, The Ronald Press Company, 1964. New York, N.Y., p. 388.

[32]*Ibid.*, pp. 389-390.

[33]Abrahamson, Stephen, "Professional Education," *Review of Educational Research*, Volume XXXV, Number 4, October 1965, p. 336.

[34]*Ibid.*, p. 336.

CHAPTER 8
Adult Education and
Continuing Education

ADULT EDUCATION, college extension courses, home study services, correspondence courses, and radio and television programs have exhibited the tendency to expand knowledge far beyond the narrow confines of the college campus. This is as it should be today.

Figure 8-1 illustrates the type of school attended by persons 35 and older:

FIGURE 8—1
Type of school attended by persons 35 and older,
by sex and race, October 1972 (in thousands) [1]

	Total	Elementary/ high school	College Full time	Part time	Trade or vocational
Both sexes	1,458	6.9%	9.1%	45%	39.1%
Men	710	6.3	10.8	41	41.8
Women	748	7.4	7.4	48.8	36.5
White	1,289	5	8.4	45.7	40.9
Black and other races	169	20.7	14.2	39.6	25.4

Source: U.S. Department of Labor.

U.S. Park Ranger John Krisko is among nearly 1.5 million Americans 35 years old and over who have returned to school for either a degree or further job training.

A Bureau of Labor Statistics study has found that one in 50 adults in the age group is using his spare time to attend school. Data for the labor force report was gathered as part of the October, 1972, Current Population Survey. Included are persons enrolled in elementary; high school; college; graduate school; or enrolled in professional studies in business, trade, or vocational schools.

The survey confined its study to those going to school to earn a degree or to train for an occupation. Outside its compass were "millions of persons flocking to classes" in the arts and practical courses in home and auto maintenance, which are not designed for career development or professional advancement.

Like Krisko, many adults are studying to keep up with new developments in their chosen fields, the survey showed. Still others want to get the necessary credentials to enter a new line of work.

Some are housewives taking college courses to obtain an under-graduate or graduate degree before reentering the labor market. Others are workers who seek a high school diploma or college degree.

When the study was made, more than half the adults in school were attending college and graduate school. Nearly two-fifth were attending trade and vocational schools. The remainder were attending elementary or high schools.

Three-fourths of the adult students surveyed also remained in the labor force, using their leisure time to attend classes.

Such services as we have indicated should be available to all American citizens. Individuals sixty-five years of age and over (Senior Citizens) should be enabled to take ALL courses, free of charge (including texts and other materials as may be needed).

Engaging in such activity will assist America in three ways, namely: (1) Will increase the productivity of each individual's contribution to society; (2) Will increase the gross national income of our nation and (3) Will decrease the public welfare rolls and unemployment without our country. There is no reason for any human being to be forced into retirement if he is still physically and mentally able to carry on in a normal manner. For those who may be handicapped mentally, physically, etc., retiring under proper guidance and supervision is perhaps the only alternative at the moment.

America needs the combined unity of all Americans regardless of race, creed, nationality, or place of residence. To work at a career in late life has the tendency to spur people, to enlighten them, and motivate them to see life in a new light. This is the VISION that all should pursue. The GOOD SOCIETY is obtainable, if our Nation is willing to seek new ways and paths to solve the multiplicity of problems. And, no individual, or group can see this through an independent endeavor; to realize this goal, cooperation and joint-action is necessary.

1"Time card and report card: Many adults are getting both," *Chicago Tribune*, Sunday, February 10, 1974, Section 12, p. 37.

✿
CHAPTER 9
Articulation in Education

IN ORDER TO ascertain the effectiveness of our educational system, we need some tools which will tell us whether or not we are actually achieving what we think we are doing. After all, youth attending our schools are bound to be affected emotionally, socially, physically, mentally, and spiritually. To what effect then, are we realizing the educational objectives society would like to achieve?

The author proposes at this interim — the use of *articulation* criteria. This system of evaluation is valid, reliable and easy to administer and interpret. Let us see just exactly what *articulation* is all about.

Articulation may be defined as the *efficient* progress made by a student in our educational system. By *efficiency* we mean that each student is able to progress from one grade to another using his maximal potential aptitude with no major obstacles impeding his efforts, needs, interests and aspirations. This is an example of good articulation, or coordination of his unique capacities.

Articulation is something like a good grade oil. It may be used in all makes of cars, a Rolls Royce, Pontiac, or Fiat. With an adequate amount of oil in the motor of a car, it will run efficiently; let the oil level drop below a certain mark and the motor is headed for trouble.

We have arrived at the point in education today where the "quality of instruction" must be commensurate with the needs of society. Quality of instruction is defined in many varied ways. The writer would like to propose that we view the "quality of instruction" as the activities and experiences provided by the teacher. In order that these activities and experiences be of utmost importance, certain behavioral changes are necessary in youth. Whatever behavioral changes the teacher may think adequate (in terms of the educational objectives to be achieved) the teacher must FIRST gain the respect and confidence of the individual, or the group.

Anything done by an instructor to cause the students to be challenged by the subject studied, to create a better understanding, to develop better work-study-habits, attitudes and appreciation — whatever is done by the teacher to extend youth these opportunities is articulation.

Articulation may be the cumulative record of a particular student. If all teachers were to study the cumulative record at the beginning of the school year for each student to be taught in classwork, the teacher would gain a better understanding of the *strengths* as well as *limitations* of the students. A profile made of the class as to its level of aptitude, achievement, special interests, needs, character and personality traits as might be indicated by standardized tests and inventory scales, interviews, etc., would undoubtedly enable the instructor to do a better job of teaching. We are assuming at this point that the more information an instructor may have about the students he is to teach, the better prepared he should be to teach effectively and at the level of each student in class.

Articulation then may be a host of different things, namely: a visit to a student's home, a personal conference with the student and/or the parent, a particular method of pedagogy, an audio-visual aid, the tape recorder, an oral or written test, an open or closed book examination. Articulation then may be seen to take the shape of many things, but in the last analysis, it is the coordination of the varied teaching phases which occur between the student and the teacher.

Articulation is like electricity — a force which tends to produce a positive action between the teacher and the potential learner. The *strength* of articulation may be rated by the instructor *observing* the student's attitude, interest, understanding and creativity.

Again, articulation may be similar to electricity, that is, the attraction exerted between two opposite poles (teacher versus the student). Or, expressed another way, articulation or electricity may be measured by the current or flow of results, or reactions it produces in a circuit having a definite resistance (again, student-teacher relationship — either may be a resistant force).

Thus, the absolute unit of articulation may be defined as *all* areas in a school situation which will exert some effect on the student's progress. A group of concentric circles may better illustrate our idea along this line. See Figure 9-1.

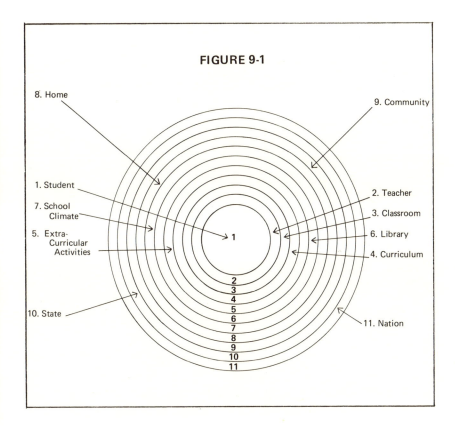

FIGURE 9-1

8. Home

9. Community

1. Student

2. Teacher

7. School Climate

3. Classroom

5. Extra-Curricular Activities

6. Library

4. Curriculum

1

2
3
4
5
6
7
8
9
10
11

10. State

11. Nation

In reviewing Figure 9-1, one may note the various areas which bombard the student and his teacher each day class is in session. Not mentioned are additional factors which may modify, accelerate, or retard the student's school progress, namely: living conditions at home; socio-economic problems of the family; the number of siblings or the absence of this relationship, separation of parents; standards of the home, school and the community; the impact of the church in the community and the various pressures coming from county, state, and federal agencies. These factors are not intended to be complete in any manner — merely suggestive of the potential persuasive tendencies as may be found which may affect the progress of the student. Any such impediment restricting the normal progress of youth in educational classroom situations might be characterized as faulty articulation.

If administration of a school system is functioning efficiently, articulation is being carried out in a satisfactory manner. If any of the areas as listed in Figure 9-1 are present and offer resistance to the teacher and/or the student, by resistance we mean, opposition to the desired goals of instruction, the normal progress of the student will be thwarted.

Horizontal and Vertical Articulation

Horizontal articulation refers to all the teachers on the same grade level. For example, all teachers in the same grade, but teaching different sections (honors group, above average, average, or below average sections) should be cognizant as to what direction each teacher may be heading. A department of English consisting of some 8 to 16 faculty members should embrace some common agreement as to what the faculty may suggest as guiding policies for retention, acceleration, promotion, honors classes, grading practices, ability grouping, educational objectives, activities and experiences to be provided youth, guidance and counseling techniques, evaluation procedures, etc.

Vertical articulation refers to the various levels through which a student passes in our educational system. For example, moving from third to fourth grade, or from tenth to the eleventh grade, or from undergraduate to graduate level work is an example of vertical coordination. A teacher in the third grade should know what standards may be required by the fourth grade teacher, or how could she possibly prepare her students for the succeeding grade level? At the secondary level, teachers directing freshmen should certainly know (assuming these teachers teach English) what educational objectives or standards are being sponsored in the sophomore level English classes. Courses in instruction should be in *sequence* of each other and as we progress from one course to another on a higher level, we would obviously assume the requirements, or standards, would be continually more demanding and exacting. Ordinarily, one thinks that the college is a bit more sophisticated than the high school, but, this assumption is not always true as will be illustrated later in this chapter.

Integrative Articulation

A third type of articulation may be characterized as *integrative.* This type of articulation may be explained by resorting to an example in the teaching of swimming.

In teaching a beginner how to swim, a coach is interested in exposing the student to three fundamentals, namely: (1) Leg movements, (2) Arm movements and (3) Breathing.

After the student has mastered all three fundamentals, the next step is to coordinate these three fundamentals, or integrate these movements. The most capable students appear to master this *integrative articulation* very easily. While some students are able to perform each fundamental in excellent fashion, they sometimes experience difficulty in articulating these functions. This might be caused by many different factors, some of which may be physiological, neurological, poor reaction time, lack of motivation, etc.

In similar fashion, a teacher teaching a group how to spell correctly has to introduce the word, pronounce the word, define it, and then use it in a sentence. The group then moves through the same procedure as the teacher. Or, a sentence or phrase may be read in class and students may then ask questions. At this point, a dictionary comes in mighty handy. A class discussion may then resolve the meaning of words heretofore never used or spoken by the students.

If pupils are taught the details effectively and the assignment seemingly challenges youth, these students will invariably carry out their own *integrative articulation* with little, or no prodding by the instructor.

The term *articulation* if carried out properly by teachers and administrators can discard many of the forces and conditions that are influencing poor learning performance on the part of students. For example, the primary purpose of administration is to facilitate instruction. If administration cannot do this, then there is no alternative but to abandon administration. Some administrators do not understand this responsibility. As a result, the faculty is left floundering guided by no sensible educational direction whatsoever. Many administrators have little or no understanding of the difficulties and obstacles to which teachers are exposed when they are asked to carry out major innovations or experimental tasks within a given school system.

Articulation is concerned with every movement in the learning process. For example, the attitudes of teachers and teacher expectations influence the performance of children. Overlooking the attitudes of teachers could in many cases be the basic reason for pupils not being able to read at a particular grade level. The climate of a school may be a factor triggering other elements which when combined serve as impedimenta in the child's progress in educational situations.

The author has developed *articulation criteria* which may be used to evaluate the "quality of instruction" of a school system. These evaluative articulation criteria appear to have an omnipotent power. For example, it makes little difference where they are used — whether it is Alaska, Siberia, Australia, India, or China — the results are comparable. For instance, teachers in India are attempting to develop character traits in their youth just as they are in other parts of the world; teachers in India, China, Russia, or elsewhere are desirous that their youth learn something about cooperating with their fellow-men, how to respect the dignity and individuality of their peers, how to assimilate self-control and willingness to accept constructive criticism. These same concepts are part and parcel of educational programs wherever one may roam. The only difference between the programs is the pathway which may be followed by a nation in order to achieve this desired characteristic, or end goal. WHO IS TO SAY THAT ONE EDUCATIONAL SYSTEM IS SUPERIOR TO ANOTHER? SUPERIOR TO WHAT?

From what we have stated thus far, the reader should have this understanding of "articulation." Articulation is similar to the spokes in a wheel. *No spokes, no circumference or wheel.* Further, articulation is the *prerequisite* prior to the functioning of accountability. Articulation represents the coordinating elements necessary to teach, select the content for subject matter teaching, to design the educational objectives, promote activities and experiences which will challenge youth and in the varied techniques of evaluation. UNLESS ALL OF THESE ACTIVITIES ARE COORDINATED BY MEANS OF ARTICULATION, THE FUNCTIONS OF ACCOUNTABILITY WILL BE DIMINISHED IN VALUE.

To see how these "articulation criteria" actually function, let us turn to the next chapter where the author has unveiled a national survey covering elementary and secondary schools, colleges and universities.

✿
CHAPTER 10
Articulation in Public and Private Educational Systems

THE PROGRAM of education in the United States is arranged in a number of separate units such as the nursery school, the kindergarten, elementary school, secondary school, and the college or university. This arrangement is supposed to provide a vehicle whereby pupils are assigned to these areas according to their level of maturity and stage of achievement. This classification of areas resembles a ladder where each rung leads directly to the next. Theoretically, at least, this represents a system in which the educational units are supposedly carefully articulated. The American Association of School Administrators in their *Seventh Yearbook* (1929) defined articulation as "that adequate relation of part to part which makes for continuous forward movement."

A child may progress in the American educational ladder by passing satisfactorily through the various unit levels, or the student may move foreward in terms of educational goals (competencies and skills) as taught in the several areas.

We may further state that articulation presumably exists between the various units of the educational system for at least two basic reasons, namely: (1) School officials promote economy by exercising purposeful articulation — if the pupils are thwarted periodically in their progress, the system may be described as being inefficient so far as the educational organization may be concerned; and (2) the necessity for effective articulation is stimulated by the democratic ideals fostered by the American people. For example, in the United

States, each citizen is permitted to progress in accordance with his capabilities. If, perchance, the school organization features blocks to a student's progress which prohibit the pupil to accomplish all that he is capable of achieving, then we may assume that the school system has failed to meet the ideals of our democratically organized society.

As the problems of articulation and of all the individuals involved in it multiply, so also does the need for information. Never before has there been a greater need for assistance, in the form of usable knowledge, in decision-making.

Purpose of Study

To investigate the possible behavioral characteristics as they may be associated with program articulation among elementary and secondary schools, colleges and universities, both public and private, a study was conducted during the 1967-68 academic year.

Specifically, eleven probable factors comprised the nucleus of this study, namely: (1) The goals to be achieved by teachers in subject matter; (2) Duplication of subject matter; (3) Attitudes of teachers; (4) Articulation between the elementary school and the college or university; (5) College entrance requirements; (6) Cooperation between home and school; (7) Teaching personnel and their comprehension of the total educational process; (8) Preparation of teachers; (9) Standards of promotion and advancement from one grade level to the next grade level; (10) Geographical areas served by the schools, and (11) The cumulative record.

Sampling Population

An opinionnaire was forwarded during the Fall session of 1967-68 academic year to approximately 1000 elementary schools, 800 secondary schools, and 500 colleges and universities. Both public and private schools were represented at each of the three levels. The schools were selected on a random basis from Education Directories as published and distributed by the State Department of Education of each state. Colleges and universities were selected from the regional accreditation association brochures.

The number of actual respondents who voluntarily participated for each level was:568 elementary schools (57 percent response), 615 secondary schools (77 percent response), and 360 colleges and universities (72 percent response). Out of a total of nearly 1,500 degree-granting institutions in the United States no less than 1,173 are reported as offering teacher education programs,[1] hence the 360 colleges and universities in this particular study represents about 30 percent of the total number existing in the United States.

Combining the data, some 1,543 educational institutions are represented in this study and reflect the opinions of 41 states. The total number of respondents representing faculty members who returned the opinionnaire numbered 4,884.[2,3]

Treatment of Data

To enable faculty participants to express their attitudes in a candid manner, no signature was required on the opinionnaire. The respondent merely indicated his or her status by placing an X in the proper box provided in the opinionnaire, for example, whether elementary, secondary, college or university.

Each participant was asked to evaluate eleven statements using the *Blanchard Index of Efficiency*. For example, the index is illustrated as follows:

BLANCHARD INDEX OF EFFICIENCY

Poor	Weak	Good	Superior	Exceptional
1	2	3	4	5

Three groups of teaching personnel were involved in using the *Blanchard Index of Efficiency*, namely: elementary teachers, secondary teachers, and college or university faculty members. Each of the 4,884 participants evaluated eleven statements (articulation criteria) as related to the level to which they were assigned to teach. For example, if a secondary school teacher rated a statement of being WEAK within his school system, a numerical score of 2 was indicated by placing an X on the broken line just below the number 2. If an instructor rated a statement as being between GOOD and SUPERIOR, an X was placed on the continuous line between the numerical numbers of 3 and 4 indicating the rating was 3.5. This was the *first* stage of faculty participation.

In the *second* stage, faculty members were asked: "What suggestions would you propose to improve conditions?" While many ideas were suggested, ONLY those proposals for improving conditions were included which, when tabulated, indicated a "frequency of mention" of 200 or above. Ideas thus suggested by faculty members were categorized thus falling into a certain division or class of proposals.

In the *third* stage, all scores for each level, namely: elementary, secondary, college or university, were averaged and the mean score was computed. The standard deviation of each mean score was computed as this would indicate to some degree, the stability of the mean score.

In the *fourth* and final stage, a Pearson r between elementary (1) versus secondary (2), elementary (1) versus college or university (3), and secondary (2) versus college and university (3) ratings were computed. By combining the correlations by means of Fischer's *z function*, a mean correlation resulted thus indicating the degree of relationship existing between the raters.

At this point then, let us review the results of one such statement, or as the author suggests, an important *articulation criterion*. If the reader wishes a more detailed review of this national survey, the monograph as published by the University of Dayton should be secured.

The three groups of faculty members were asked the question: WITH RESPECT TO A COMMON UNDERSTANDING OF THE GOALS TO BE ACHIEVED IN TEACHING, HOW WOULD YOU RATE THE TEACHERS WITHIN YOUR SCHOOL SYSTEM?

FIGURE 10-1
Ratings of Teachers as to Goals to be Achieved

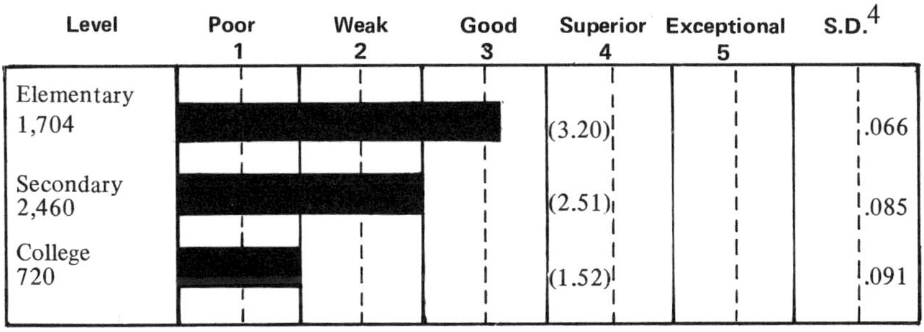

Level	Poor 1	Weak 2	Good 3	Superior 4	Exceptional 5	S.D.[4]
Elementary 1,704				(3.20)		.066
Secondary 2,460			(2.51)			.085
College 720		(1.52)				.091

According to Figure 10-1, the elementary teachers are rated 3.20, or slightly better than GOOD pertaining to a common understanding of the goals to be achieved in teaching; secondary teaching personnel are rated 2.51, or midway between WEAK and GOOD, and college instructors earned a rating of 1.52, which is about midway between POOR and WEAK.

One of the persistent problems in education which seemingly accents the loss of articulation in a given subject is apparently due to the different emphases rendered by teachers to various learning situations through which the pupil passes. In each area, as illustrated in Figure 10-1, the elementary, secondary and college levels indicate a high degree of mediocrity. In short, instructional personnel do not exhibit a healthy understanding of the goals to be achieved in teaching. If this may be assumed to be true, one may cast serious doubt upon the value of the activities planned by teachers for the students.

A tentative conclusion which might be inferred at this point: It appears that elementary teachers have a greater common understanding of the goals to be sought in teaching than either secondary or college level teaching personnel. If this lack of articulation, or uneven progress in single subjects is so pronounced, what deductions may one draw relative to subjects of a sequential nature, for example, Arithmetic I, Arithmetic II, Arithmetic III, or History I, II, III, etc.?

In answer to the question: "What suggestions would you propose to improve conditions?" the following answers are listed according to their rank order of importance:

Level answering:	Response
	"I think we lack the proper educational leadership."
Elementary and Secondary	"The supervisory program has not been worked out cooperatively."
	"We should have in-service training program relative to curriculum planning and development."
College	"Elementary, secondary and college levels should meet periodically to discuss problems of articulation.
	"Consultants from each level might interchange and pool ideas. This joint-action might assist in solving articulation problems."
	"Teacher training institutions might provide opportunities in undergraduate and graduate study whereby all 3 levels might work together on a common problem."

Another way we can express the rating given by elementary, secondary and college instructors would be to determine the coefficient of correlation between the ratings. Hence, let us denote 1 = elementary; 2 = secondary, and 3 = college. Therefore, if we correlate 1 vs. 2, 1 vs. 3, and 2 vs. 3, we have Figure 10-2:

FIGURE 10–2

LEVEL	N	r	LEVEL OF SIGNIFICANCE
1 vs. 2	600	.82	< .001
1 vs. 3	600	.78	< .001
2 vs. 3	600	.76	< .001
Combining 1, 2 and 3 by Fischer's Z function			
		.79	< .001

Reviewing Figure 10-2, one may note that in the rating of this particular characteristic (articulation criterion), a high degree of relationship exists between elementary, secondary and college level teachers. While the individual correlations range from .76 to .82 and significant at the < .001 level, the combined mean r is equal to .79 and significant at the < .001 level.

What this means briefly is just this: Teachers at every level of the American educational system are in agreement that they lack a common understanding of the goals to be achieved in teaching. Can we single out just ONE reason as to why this should exist? The writer believes that there is one basic cause for this malpractice and that is, that it is *not* the fault of the elementary or the secondary schools within this country, but it is *primarily* the fault of institutions of higher education engaged in preparing candidates for a teaching career. IT IS IMPOSSIBLE TO TRAIN PROSPECTIVE TEACHERS WITH JUST TWO YEARS OF SPECIALIZED AND PROFESSIONAL GUIDANCE. And, this is just what is happening and will continue to operate, unless some specific action is taken by the proper authorities.

Imagine a doctor of medicine given the same amount of training attempting to practice surgery or administering to individual human ailments! The undertakers and embalmers in this country would welcome such an innovation.

Under the plan suggested by the writer in the re-structuring of our educational system, candidates preparing for a teaching career would have TWICE the amount of training they secure today. We cannot cure the ills of poor quality teaching until we change the requirements fostered in higher education. Students need the first year in college for *observation* purposes in the various levels of our educational system; the first year of college should additionally afford each prospective teacher the opportunity to serve under a seasoned warrior to feel the pulse of a teaching career — to sense his own personal limitations and weaknesses as well as strengths. An overview of every program by the student is necessary prior to his launching in this complex area of teaching. During this first year, the prospective teacher can begin his course work in specialization and professional courses.

Under the plan proposed by the author, student teaching would become equivalent to the internship served by a candidate for the doctor of medicine degree. Each teacher candidate would serve a full year, preferably the fourth year, under the supervision of a master teacher carrying on a program comparable to a regularly employed teacher. The teacher candidate would receive a salary along somewhat the same lines as provided the medical internship. THIS TYPE OF TRAINING IS ESSENTIAL IF WE ARE INTERESTED IN IMPROVING THE QUALITY OF INSTRUCTION!

The current student teaching assignments might be labelled a *farce* as it is carried on today. Little, if any, significant evaluation of the student is planned or structured so as to be meaningful to the amateur teacher. It might be better to abandon student teaching altogether as it is administered today and permit the student to take additional subject matter. At least, this would be an improvement — until the writer's plan is put into effect.

How to Rank Your High School

Now that the reader has had the opportunity to review the discussions relative to articulation criteria, let us see how a high school might be rated using these techniques. During the Fall of 1973, the writer handpicked the "TOP TEN" secondary schools in the United States. This marks the FIRST time any secondary school has been evaluated with these articulation criteria. The "TOP TEN" high schools in the country today are:

1. Maine Township High School, Park Ridge, Illinois.
2. Peabody Senior High School, Pittsburgh, Pennsylvania.
3. Muskegon Senior High School, Muskegon, Michigan.
4. Paul Laurence Dunbar High School, Dayton, Ohio.
5. Houston High School, San Antonio, Texas.
6. Casa Grande High School, Case Grande, Arizona.
7. Wade Hampton High School, Greenville, South Carolina.
8. Capitol Senior High School, East Baton, Louisiana.
9. Grant High School, Portland, Oregon.
10. Morgantown High School, Morgantown, West Virginia.

The following articulation instrument was used to select the "TOP TEN" secondary schools. For those desiring to evaluate their own school, the following is presented:

INSTRUCTIONS:

Instruct teachers to read each statement carefully and to evaluate their colleagues on a scale from 1 to 5 (poor to exceptional).

(SAMPLE SCALE)

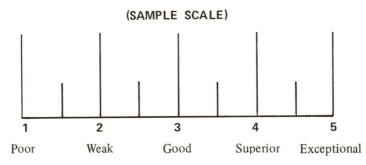

1	2	3	4	5
Poor	Weak	Good	Superior	Exceptional

Tabulate by adding the scores for each statement, then dividing the sum by the number of respondents.

Keep in mind that the very nature of a norm dictates that half of all responses will be below the norm and half above. Schools that are average or below may indeed be doing commendable work, considering their individual circumstances.

The articulation criteria used for selecting the "TOP TEN" secondary schools in the United States are concerned primarily with the *quality of instruction.*[6]

	Your Norm	Nat'l Norm	Top 10 Norm

1. Rate the teachers in your school on their common understanding of the goals to be achieved in teaching.

1 2 3 4 5 | 2.51 | 4.27

2. Rate your school on articulation of specific subject matter from grade to grade. (Are all teachers working cooperatively to prepare students adequately for each succeeding grade level?)

1 2 3 4 5 | 1.94 | 4.15

3. Rate the attitudes of teachers toward the work of the elementary or junior high schools from which you draw your students.

1 2 3 4 5 | 2.50 | 4.36

4. Rate the degree of articulation between junior and senior high or elementary and secondary school in the following areas:

a. curriculum

1 2 3 4 5 | 3.65 | 4.73

b. Educational objectives

1 2 3 4 5 | 2.50 | 4.61

c. Methods of instruction

1 2 3 4 5 | 2.40 | 4.80

d. Activities provided for students

1 2 3 4 5 | 2.60 | 4.39

e. Evaluation

1 2 3 4 5 | 1.75 | 4.55

5. Rate the effect of current college entrance requirements on your school's curriculum. (Do teachers pay proper attention to student interests, not subjugating them to college subject matter requirements?)

1 2 3 4 5 | 1.50 | 2.81

6. Rate the cooperation between your school and the home of the student.

1 2 3 4 5 | 1.52 | 4.13

7. Rate teachers on their comprehension of the total educational system. (Does the ninth-grade English teacher know what the tenth grade English teacher may require of the student? Do teachers know what their colleagues on the elementary level are concerned about?)

1 2 3 4 5 | 2.20 | 4.29

8. Rate the type of educational preparation you received as an undergraduate headed for a teaching career.

1 2 3 4 5 | 2.65 | 3.78

9. Rate whether the standards of promotion and advancement from one grade level to the next are equally understood by all teachers, parents and students.

1 2 3 4 5 | 1.40 | 4.46

10. Rate your school on planning orientation programs or providing proper transitional phases for new students or students who transfer from one department to another.

1 2 3 4 5 | 2.40 | 4.53

11. Rate the cumulative student record system used in your school. (Do teachers fill out these records adequately and use them frequently as valuable sources of information on needs and interests of individual students?)

1 2 3 4 5 | 2.50 | 4.34

Overall norm (add each of your norms listed above and divide by 15)[5]

2.27 | 4.28

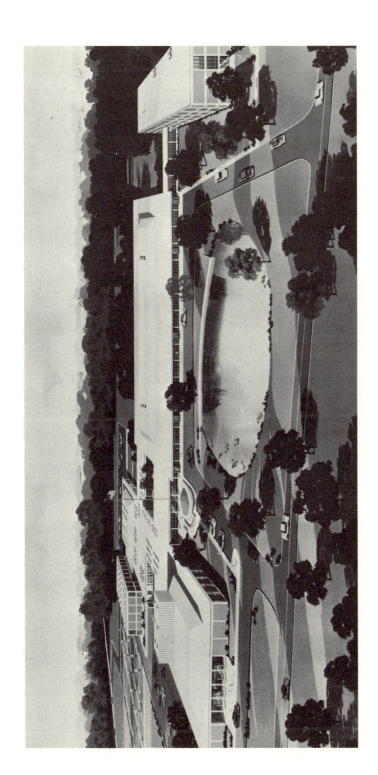

MAINE TOWNSHIP HIGH SCHOOL, Park Ridge, Illinois

PEABODY SENIOR HIGH SCHOOL, Pittsburgh, Pennsylvania

MUSKEGON SENIOR HIGH SCHOOL, Muskegon, Michigan

CASA GRANDE HIGH SCHOOL, Casa Grande, Arizona

U.S. GRANT HIGH SCHOOL, Portland, Oregon

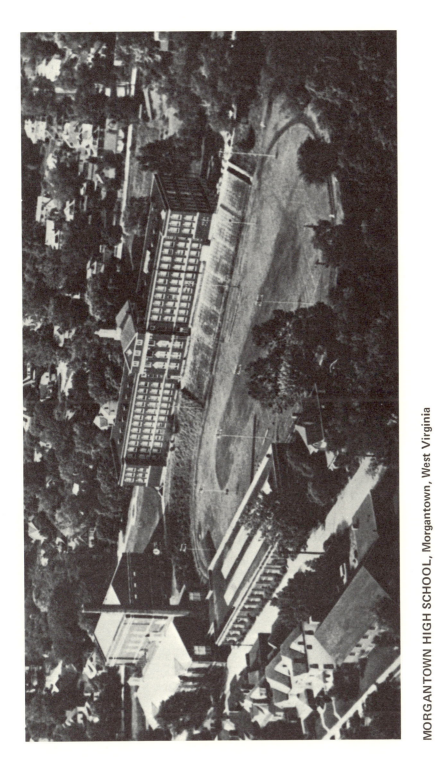

MORGANTOWN HIGH SCHOOL, Morgantown, West Virginia

Since high schools exist for the purpose of providing instruction, we next need teachers to provide this type of information. From the author's point of view, the most important function served by either faculties of secondary schools or undergraduate colleges, is the *teaching function*. If this can be assumed to be true, let's evaluate what is most important, namely, TEACHING! The sole reason for the writer directing a national survey in the area of articulation was to find out if articulation criteria might effectively evaluate the *teaching* function. The author firmly and unequivocally believes that adhering to the use of such criteria will enable schools to evaluate themselves in a much more critical fashion than using the time-worn guidelines provided by current regional accreditation associations.

Rating Colleges by Articulation Studies[7]

Taking a random sampling of some 360 colleges and universities as indicated in a previous chapter (University of Dayton monograph), the author selected the "TOP THIRTY" colleges and universities in the country today. These institutions of higher education are as follows: See Figure 10-3.

In reviewing Figure 10-3, one may note that the top institution of higher education in the United States today is Bowdoin College of Brunswick, Maine. This outstanding and distinguished liberal arts college with approximately 1000 students recently set a milestone in the history of American education when its faculty voted to eliminate the College Board examination requirement for admissions candidates.

Bowdoin College considers admissions a match-making process: our College is not necessarily right for every good student, and every good student is not necessarily right for Bowdoin.[8]

The second top ranking institution of higher education is the National College of Education located in Evanston, Illinois. The educational leadership, faculty morale, student body, alumni, interested patrons of the College and the Board of Trustees are to be commended for their ability to work cooperatively and in joint-action to satisfy the goals of the College which might be expressed in one word, namely — EXCELLENCE.

The pendulum of "quality education" appears to have shifted from the East and West to the Midwest, if articulation standards

FIGURE 10–3
Rating Colleges by Articulation Studies

INSTITUTION OF HIGHER EDUCATION	RATING
Bowdoin College, Brunswick, Maine	4.39
National College of Education, Evanston, Illinois	4.35
University of Illinois, Urbana, Illinois	4.03
Greenville College, Greenville, Illinois	3.95
New York University, Washington Square, New York City	3.91
McKendree College, Lebanon, Illinois	3.85
Illinois State University, Normal, Illinois	3.80
University of Chicago, Chicago, Illinois	3.78
North Park College, Chicago, Illinois	3.73
De Paul University, Chicago, Illinois	3.69
Marquette University, Milwaukee, Wisconsin	3.67
Duke University, Durham, North Carolina	3.63
Bowling Green State University, Bowling Green, Ohio . .	3.60
Elmhurst College, Elmhurst, Illinois.	3.58
Shimer College, Mount Carroll, Illinois	3.58
Tolentine College, Olympia Fields, Illinois.	3.57
Illinois College, Jacksonville, Illinois	3.47
University of Dayton, Dayton, Ohio	3.46
Augustana College, Rock Island, Illinois	3.44
Loyola University, New Orleans, Louisiana	3.42
Barat College, Lake Forest, Illinois	3.40
Arizona State University, Tempe, Arizona	3.38
Trinity College, Deerfield, Illinois.	3.36
Boston College, Chestnut Hill, Massachusetts.	3.35
University of Oregon, Eugene, Oregon	3.33
Mundelein College, Chicago, Illinois	3.30
Carroll College, Helena, Montana	3.27
Western Michigan University, Kalamazoo, Michigan	3.24
University of Pennsylvania, Philadelphia, Pennsylvania	3.17
Eastern Illinois University, Charleston, Illinois	3.14

Dr. Roger Howell, Jr., President of Bowdoin, has maintained this College's cherished tradition of administrators who are also scholars and teachers. President Howell is shown here at the head of the table conducting a History seminar. (Reproduced by permission of Mr. Joseph D. Kamin, Director of News Services, Bowdoin College, Brunswick, Maine.

Bowdoin winter scene. The building is the Hawthorne-Longfellow Library, completed in 1965 and named after the two literary giants who were both members of Bowdoin's Class of 1825.

can be accepted as valid criteria. The "hub" or focal point of this elite education is centered in . . . ILLINOIS. It may be noted that of the "TOP TEN" institutions of higher education, eight are Midwest Illinois schools.

Justification for Articulation Criteria

There are undoubtedly well-known figures in professional education who might object to the use of articulation criteria in evaluating public and private schools, colleges or universities. To these individuals, the author wishes to reply as follows:

1. In each case of directing evaluation surveys thus far, the writer has used articulation criteria which are DIRECTLY related to the teaching process.
2. Articulation criteria are different than those proposed as standards, or guidelines by regional accrediting associations. An articulation factor is one which coordinates several actions into one or more end goal. For example, a teacher may have excellent training in subject matter, but lacks the proper *attitude*, hence her resultant teaching may be totally ineffective as far as the learning process is concerned. Any little thing, or series of things, a teacher may do to *challenge* the student is a *functioning* articulation criterion or criteria.
3. The self-studies as utilized by the writer in gaining the reaction of faculty members to the varied articulation criteria, is to some extent, comparable to the self-study reports which public and private schools, colleges and universities *must* submit to the accrediting associations. This self-study is generally regarded as a valuable and helpful experience, indicating to the faculty and administration the strengths and weaknesses of the teacher education program.
4. A personal evaluation by a school system may sometimes be more *enlightening* and *purposeful* than having a visiting committee from a regional or national accrediting agency evaluate the host institution.
5. Using articulation criteria as suggested by the writer enables an institution of learning the opportunity to assess itself at any time deemed desirable. And the articulation criteria can be modified, changed, or discarded for newly proposed articulation criteria as worked out cooperatively by faculty, students and the administration.

[1] Mayor, John R., and Swartz, Willis G. *Accreditation in Teacher Education: Its Influence on Higher Education.* National Commission on Accrediting, 1785 Massachusetts Avenue N.W., Washington, D.C. 20036. p. 86.

[2] Blanchard, B. Everard. *Behavioral Characteristics Peculiar to Articulation in American Educational Programs.* (A monograph). Published and distributed by Education Research Center, School of Education, University of Dayton, Dayton, Ohio, 1972, p. 3.

[3] The 4,884 equals 1,704 faculty members of the elementary school; 2,460 faculty members of the secondary school and 720 faculty members representing colleges and universities.

[4] S.D. refers to the Standard Deviation.

[5] Blanchard, B. Everard, "How to rank your high school," *The Nation's Schools*, Vol. 93, No. 2, February 1974, pp. 46-47.

[6] Blanchard, B. Everard, "Who'll Name the 'TOP TEN' High Schools in the U.S.?" *The American School Board Journal*, Vol. 161, No. 1, pp. 26-29.

[7] Sodomka, Dennis, "Rating Colleges by Articulation Studies," *The National Observer*, Week Ending July 28, 1973, p. 10.

[8] Personnel communication from Dr. Richard W. Moll, Director of Admissions, Bowdoin College, Brunswick, Maine.

CHAPTER 11
A Zero Occupation:
National and Regional
Accrediting Associations

I N 1931, Samuel P. Capen, speaking on "The Principles Which Should Govern Standards and Accrediting Practices," said, that there are *no* principles, and further:

> I believe there should no longer be any accrediting practices. If tomorrow morning every accrediting committee in the country should adjourn *sine die* and every accredited list should be destroyed, I believe American Education would receive such a stimulus as it has not received in a dozen years.[1]

Henry M. Wriston, President Emeritus of Brown University in writing a letter under the title, "The Futility of Accrediting," stated:

> The accrediting procedure does not protect us from the wretched and fraudulent institutions and that the pursuit of excellence is not advanced by accrediting procedures.[2]

The regional accrediting associations came into being at the turn of the century for the simple reason that colleges were not adequately prepared to accept the graduates of various high schools, for example:

The North Central Association was called into being to meet some of the critical problems facing education in the Middle West as a result of the significant changes in . . . the educational enterprise . . . (near) the turn of the century . . . Established colleges, faced with applications for admission from graduates of a bewildering array of secondary schools, found themselves without standards by which to judge the qualifications of the applicants.[3]

The contemporary demands for evaluation are greater today than they have ever been in the history of education. Mr. John Q. Public wants to see colleges and universities rated. *The Chronicle of Higher Education* notes that some 21 governmental agencies ask for some assurance relative to the quality of colleges before they will grant funds for building programs or research[4] and members of the various state legislatures want some degree of assurance that educational institutions are using funds prudently and producing acceptable products.

The author has proposed a new method of evaluating elementary schools, high schools, colleges and universities by means of *articulation criteria* (discussed in an earlier chapter) which is valid, reliable, economical and easily interpreted.[5]

Why Accrediting Associations Should be Abolished

For one thing, there is a great deal of *overlapping* between the State Department of Education, the North Central Association and the National Council for Accreditation of Teacher Education. The standards and guidelines provided by each of the three groups as mentioned are decidedly comparable.

The cost of operation for these agencies is a cumbersome *monetary impact* which hits Mr. John Q. Public every year. Millions of dollars are necessary to carry on the functions of these accrediting agencies and the time has come when the taxpayer SHOULD BE RELIEVED of such an unnecessary burden.

Accrediting agencies place too much *emphasis upon things* and *money* and not enough on the quality of the product produced by the institutions of higher education.

The author strongly advocates the *total elimination* of the National Council for Accreditation of Teacher Education and the six regional accreditation associations (Middle States Association of

Colleges and Secondary Schools; New England Association of Colleges and Secondary Schools; North Central Association of Colleges and Secondary Schools; Northwest Association of Secondary and Higher Schools; Northwest Association of Secondary and Higher Schools; Southern Association of Colleges and Schools and the Western Association of Schools and Colleges).

A casual talk with Superintendents and Principals throughout the country appears to indicate that these gentlemen have had their fill of the accreditation agencies and would welcome their immediate retirement from the scene of education. One high school the writer recently visited as a member of the regional association visiting appraisal committee indicated that the cost to their school district of the visiting members — meals, hotel accommodations, travel reimbursement, etc., was approximately $2500.

On the college and university level, the visiting committee members are generally *wined* and *dined* for the three-day visitation. They live like Kings and Queens for three days and then return to their "hovel" to wait until they are given the opportunity to visit another school which they eagerly accept like the young child attending a circus for the first time.

Another real disadvantage of the regional accrediting agencies is the fact that some of the individuals selected to carry on the evaluation are *not qualified* to do the work they are supposed to do. Imagine having an individual evaluate the library who has spent his life-time teaching subjects in the area of vocational education! Or, the Dean of a college who has specialized in elementary education and is chairing an evaluation committee in the teaching of foreign languages on the college level! This is something like saying: now that you have your doctorate in mattress-making, you are now eligible for the Presidency of Playmore University.

A New Accreditation Plan

To counteract the disadvantages of the contemporary system of regional accreditation and NCATE, the author suggests what he calls a "United States Accreditation Agency." Briefly, all the states and territorial possessions would provide three professionally trained individuals to a body which would be termed the "General

Council." In turn, this *General Council* would be supported by Specialized Advisory Groups.

The *General Council* would thus set up, under the guidance of all concerned, general policies which would assist in providing control in the accreditation of public and private schools, colleges and universities, etc. Local control would be exercised by each state in evaluating their institutions of learning on all levels. On a national basis, this would provide for a *unification* of ideas concerning the goals of our educational system.

The cost of such an operation would be considerably less than what is currently spent each year for all the regional accrediting associations and the National Council for Accreditation of Teacher Education. Figure 11-1 illustrates the new accreditation plan.

In reviewing Figure 10-1, the functions of these various sections may be described as follows:

1. Each of the states and territorial possessions will be represented in the *General Council.* An estimated three individuals might be good to start with. This would provide us with a *General Council* of approximately 150 members, more or less.
2. The *General Council* would have direct control over all phases of public and private school education. This control would be of a *general policy* nature, leaving each state the responsibility of seeing that the general policies were carefully executed.
3. The *General Council* would have Specialized Advisory Groups to advise its membership from time to time.
4. The *General Council* would provide states and territorial possessions with consultant services.
5. A *Lay Advisory Group* composed of business men, industrial groups, social, civic and fraternal organizations would be represented at this point to keep the *General Council* informed as to the public's wishes.
6. The *General Council*, through its professional membership, would provide continuous and comprehensive accreditation once every five-years. The work of accreditation would be planned in joint-action between the state and the *General Council.*
7. Overlapping and duplication of effort, standards and guidelines would be reduced to a minimum.

FIGURE 11–1
˙United States Accreditation Agency

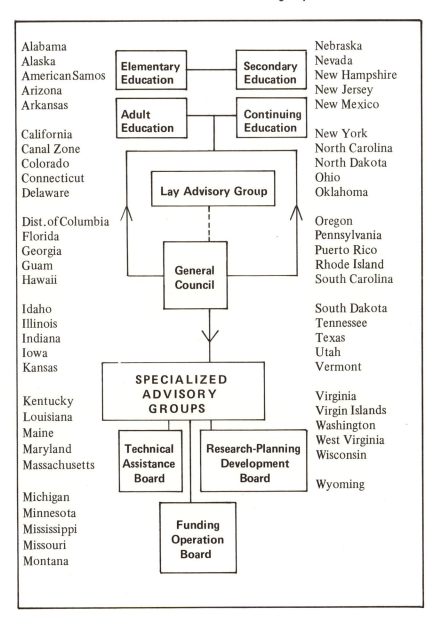

Alabama	Nebraska
Alaska	Nevada
American Samos	New Hampshire
Arizona	New Jersey
Arkansas	New Mexico
California	New York
Canal Zone	North Carolina
Colorado	North Dakota
Connecticut	Ohio
Delaware	Oklahoma
Dist. of Columbia	Oregon
Florida	Pennsylvania
Georgia	Puerto Rico
Guam	Rhode Island
Hawaii	South Carolina
Idaho	South Dakota
Illinois	Tennessee
Indiana	Texas
Iowa	Utah
Kansas	Vermont
Kentucky	Virginia
Louisiana	Virgin Islands
Maine	Washington
Maryland	West Virginia
Massachusetts	Wisconsin
Michigan	Wyoming
Minnesota	
Mississippi	
Missouri	
Montana	

Elementary Education — Secondary Education

Adult Education — Continuing Education

Lay Advisory Group

General Council

SPECIALIZED ADVISORY GROUPS

Technical Assistance Board

Research-Planning Development Board

Funding Operation Board

8. Each state and territorial possession would contribute, for example, the sum of $10,000 per annum to finance the operation of the United States Accreditation Agency.

It is well-known that the several regional accrediting offices are hard pressed to maintain operating services at the present writing. Rather than perpetuate these regional bodies, the author advocates their prompt abandonment.

In all of our states, with the exception of Alaska and Hawaii, the state departments of education have what is termed a direct or statutory responsibility for certifying public school teachers. Because of this existing interrelationship between certification and accreditation, the authority to grant teaching certificates carries with it a similar responsibility to approve teacher education programs.

State departments of education need to be strengthened with more professionally trained personnel and with a professional leader at the helm who has had training and experience in educational administration, finance, educational interpretation, curriculum development, evaluation strategy and research.

Using the articulation criteria suggested by the writer, state departments of education, under the directive influence of the *General Council*, might design more elaborate articulation criteria which would include the general policies for teacher education.

The big issue in teacher education today is that with all the best research available and with incessant change taking place, there is NO common agreement as to the type of education which should become a prerequisite for the elementary teacher, the secondary teacher, or the college or university instructor. What constitutes our educational pattern for teacher education today is based almost entirely on assumptions which are archaic and ready to be buried.

What we need to do, and to do as promptly as is possible, is to carry on a scientific survey as to the type of training necessary for teaching personnel at every level of our American educational system. We simply cannot continue to rely on heresay, or opinion.

The Bureau of Educationists have to be disturbed. We cannot prepare American youth to live in the future using an educational system designed for an age that is fast disappearing, or in many cases, has already vanished.

Research on the college and university level should be directed toward the identification and unification of the ways in which institutions of higher education influence students and the forces on the campus that assist or hinder institutions of higher learning in the fulfillment of their goals. *Goals, in the final analysis, are determined by society.*

---

[1]Capen, Samuel P., "The Principles Which Should Govern Standards and Accrediting Practices," *The North Central Association Quarterly*, VI, December 1931, pp. 340-341.

[2]Wriston, Henry M., "The Futility of Accreditation," in "Accreditation in Higher Education: A Symposium," *Journal of Higher Education*, XXXI, June 1960, pp. 327-329.

[3]Pfnister, Allan O., "Accreditation in the North Central Region," *Accreditation in Higher Education*, ed. Lloyd E. Blauch, Washington, D.C., U.S. Department of Health, Education, and Welfare, 1959, p. 52-58.

[4]*The Chronicle of Higher Education*, January 15, 1973.

[5]*The National Observer*, Week Ending July 28, 1973, p. 10.

✻
CHAPTER 12
Debunking Myths in Education

AFTER NEARLY five decades of being involved in the area of education as a coach, teacher, principal and administrator in public and private schools as well as colleges and universities, the author would like to deflate some common beliefs still existing in our educational panorama.

1. ONE REACHES SENILITY AT 65 — HENCE RETIRE.
   Maintaining that mandatory retirement can be harmful to a worker's health, the American Medical Association yesterday said it would join a law-suit seeking to declare forced retirement unconstitutional.

   "Considerable medical evidence is available to indicate that the sudden cessation of productive work and earning power of an individual, caused by compulsory retirement at the chronolocigal age of 65, often leads to physical and emotional illness and premature death," the A.M.A. said.

   Citing a recent report of the Gerontological Society, the A.M.A. said, "Workers, between 60 and 75 years of age are not only proving to be capable of working in many occupations but they also actually excel younger persons because of their superior judgment, experience, and safety performance."[1]

2. LEARNING AND CULTURE IS DECLINING.
   The percentage of illiterates in the world has dropped to 34.3, according to the United Nations Educational, Scientific,

and Cultural Organization. UNESCO said that percentage is a drop from nearly 44 percent in 1950 and 40 percent in 1960 but predicted that illiteracy may not be eliminated by the end of the century.[2]

3. THERE IS A BEST METHOD OF TEACHING.
Scattered comparisons in the area of research appear to indicate that neither the initial acquisition nor the retention of learning is substantially affected by teaching method. Thus Leton (1961), in a limited comparison of lecture and group discussion in a course in child development, found NO differences that could be ascribed to the procedures used.[3]

4. COLLEGE RESEARCH AND EVALUATION FUNCTIONS LOSING EMPHASIS.
In the significant theoretical articles of 1960, there is a strong thrust toward more basic research and a structuring of research designs which will take account of the complex variables operating in a student's life.[4]

5. COLLEGE GRADES EXCELLENT PREDICTORS.
One recent study by Aiken revealed the extent to which grades are a relative and unstable indicator of scholastic ability. While the academic capability of students who entered an unnamed college increased significantly over a three-year period, the GPA's for these classes did not improve. Even though each class admitted was more gifted than the previous class in terms of scores on SAT and high school rank, the college grades earned by classes of different ability remained the same.[5]

6. COLLEGE AND UNIVERSITY SECRET PAY POLICIES PAY OFF.
Secret pay policies, a study shows, may increase an individual's discontent with his compensation and lead to lowered productivity and effectiveness, even among the managerial group.[6]

7. TEACHER EDUCATION IS EXCELLENT.
Despite all of the shared experience and endless research, we

continue to operate our educational systems without commonly
accepted agreements about what the process of teaching should
entail or what skills and knowledges are essential to teaching.[7]

8. PSYCHOLOGY AS THE FOUNDATION OF
   CURRICULUM THEORY.
   There are no laws of learning that can be taught with
   confidence.[8] There is as yet no completely worked-out system
   of learning theory that can be readily applied.[9] The time thus
   spent on teaching about learning theories and laws of learning
   may be a *complete waste* of time as for the undergraduate and
   graduate student in college or university.

9. THE SOCIAL SCIENCES AS A BASIS FOR CURRICULUM
   There is no borderline between social psychology and sociology,
   just as there is no border between the sociology and anthro-
   pology of a primitive village. Indeed, there are very few border-
   lines, very few informing postulates, around sociology as a
   study; there seems to be no discipline, no habit of mind, no
   device for the exclusion of irrelevance. The great bulk of what
   passes for sociology, not only before the public but within the
   field, is a tedious redefinition or quantification of common
   sense.[10]

10. OFF-CAMPUS EXTENSION COURSES INFERIOR
    TO ON-CAMPUS COURSES.
    Relative to the relationship between on-campus and
    off-campus extension courses, the majority of these courses,
    namely, 52 per cent display no true difference between the two
    population means as far as earned grades are concerned.[11]

11. EASTERN COLLEGES AND UNIVERSITIES EXERT THE
    GREATEST IMPACT ON EXTENSION COURSE
    INSTRUCTORS.
    Illinois appears to be the single state which bears the greatest
    impact on the teaching experience of extension course instruc-
    tors. The top ten states seemingly exerting the greatest
    influence as to where teaching experience was acquired seem
    to be the following listed in their rank order of importance:

Illinois, Pennsylvania, Nebraska, Iowa, Ohio, Michigan, Wisconsin, Minnesota, Washington, and California.[12]

12. PROGRAMS SUCH AS "HEADSTART" ARE OF NO VALUE.

For the child born into poverty, the risk of retardation is higher than for those from more affluent backgrounds. Programs such as Headstart have attempted to "intervene": to compensate such children for their handicaps through an enriched pre-school curriculum. Many researchers now believe that intervention must begin even earlier in the deprived child's life. To test this theory, a project at the Frank Porter Graham Child Development Center (FPG) is studying the effects of a long-term intervention program that begins with infants at birth.[13]

13. COLLEGE GRADUATES IGNORING BUSINESS — CONTINUING GRADUATE STUDY.

A survey of college seniors in 1973 by the *Approach 13-3; Corporation* of Knoxville, Tennessee has produced evidence of what the corporation calls "a new focus on practicality." The survey shows that 31.7 per cent of the 1973 seniors said they planned to "begin a career, start making it" immediately after graduation, compared to 21 per cent of the 1972 seniors.[14]

14. HIGH SCHOOL "COLLEGE PREPARATORY" COURSES PREPARE FOR COLLEGE.

Hundreds of reputable research studies, almost without exception, have shown that the grades earned in universities and colleges have practically *no relationship at all* to what subjects were taken in high school.[15] So what does this mean: the colleges and universities and secondary schools in this country *should* meet cooperatively and in joint-action work out a plan of study which will show some articulation, sequence of meaning and be challenging as well as motivating to prospective students.

15. THE COLLEGE DEGREE AS A SCREENING CRITERION IN BUSINESS.

Businessmen have lost confidence in the value of the college

degree as a screening device and even in the ability of the professors themselves. Sixty-two percent of the executives felt that
only a *minority* of business school faculty were capable of
relating theory to the real world. Even more significant was the
fact that 91% of the businessmen felt that it was as important
for college of business faculty members to have actual business
experience as it was for them to have a Ph.D. degree.[16]

16. COLLEGE EDUCATION ENHANCES JOB SUCCESS.
The manpower report of the President prepared by the United
States Department of Labor and transmitted to Congress in
April, 1971 made the following points based upon research in
the area of education and employment: (1) "In eight of ten
occupations, there was *no* relationship between the workers'
educational attainment and their degree of job success," and
(2) "Widely different educational requirements are used for the
same jobs."[17]

17. HIGHER EDUCATION IS RELATED
    TO EARNING POWER.
The Associated Press reported on October 5, 1972, that Dr.
Clark Kerr, Chairman of the Carnegie Commission on Higher
Education, had the following to say during a news conference
concerning a report for the Commission:

"One of the more surprising findings is that higher education
as an investment — in terms of how much it will increase a
person's earning power — is generally overrated. A parent
could do as well with a stock investment."[18]

Vernon R. Alden, in the September 1, 1971, edition of the *Wall
Street Journal*, had the following to say regarding education:

"The great American universities will have to make changes,
as even Harvard has discovered. They will be supplemented —
not superseded, by the new institutions. In the end, they will
be better off scholastically because they will acquire a voluntary
rather than an indentured student body. I believe the public is
beginning to demand value in exchange for the taxes it pays
for education, and breaking up the monopoly held by traditional colleges and universities in the granting of degrees.

But the demand has so far been mostly an expression of frustration, of a realization that the system bypasses too many people and is costly for what it provides." [19]

Our higher education programs are turning out more graduates than the economy can absorb. In many cases people are spending four years in college and are not prepared to do any specific job when they finish, asserts Edwin L. Rumpf, Director of Vocational and Technical Education of the U.S. Office of Education. [20]

18. GIFTED CHILDREN: 'MOST PAMPERED MINORITY IN EDUCATION?'

According to a report by a commission of the Department of Health, Education and Welfare, "Fewer than 4 per cent of this country's gifted and talented are being served with programs commensurate with their needs."

According to Dr. James Gallagher, Kenan Professor of education and director of the Frank Porter Graham Child Development Center at the University of North Carolina, the myths and facts surrounding the public's attitude toward gifted children may be described as follows:

MYTH — Gifted children will triumph over mediocre education programs and achieve at a superior level without special assistance.

FACT — Many children do not triumpth over mediocre education programs and achieve at a superior level without special assistance.

FACT — Many children do not triumph over adversity, resulting in an incalculable loss to society in leadership potential for the arts, sciences, government and business.

MYTH — Gifted children come from affluent, well-educated parents who represent the white suburban elite who are able to take care of themselves.

FACT — One of the greatest potential sources of gifts and talents yet untapped are children whose gifts are disguised by clothing, dialect or cultural differences.

MYTH — Helping gifted children means giving them an additional competitive advantage and will result in a lower achievement by less talented students.

FACT — Problems such as mass transportation, pollution and fuel shortage will yield only to the most sophisticated and well-trained minds.[21]

19. OUR ELEMENTARY, JUNIOR AND SENIOR HIGH SCHOOL YOUTH ARE INFERIOR MENTALLY TO YOUTH IN OTHER COUNTRIES.
Students in U.S. elementary, junior, and senior high schools did at least as well as — and, in many cases, better than — their counterparts in the schools of 19 other nations on achievement tests of science, reading, comprehension, and literature administered on a world-wide basis by the International Association for the Evaluation of Educational Achievement (IEA). The results of the testing, involving some 258,000 students and 50,000 teachers in 9,700 schools in 20 nations, were released by IEA recently.[22]

20. PROFESSIONAL RANKING DIFFERENTIATES COMPETENCY IN TEACHING.
While instructional personnel on the elementary and the secondary level are termed "teachers" or "instructors," the college level employs the terms — instructor, lecturer, assistant professor, associate professor and full professor. Why do colleges and universities employ such names? Just to be different — a pseudo type of sophism. Actually, the ONLY difference between the varied names is money. A *lecturer* receives less salary for teaching the same course a full professor may be teaching for a larger sum of money. In many cases today, one can find college teaching personnel at the lecturer, or assistant professor level directing courses of study just as effectively as the full professor — yet he is discriminated against by being placed in a *lower salary bracket*. At the public and private school level, we rarely find this type of discrimination being practiced. Instead, teachers in grades 9 through 12 receive salaries basically on the basis of having another year of experience and the amount of formal education they have acquired.

Salaries on all levels of the American educational system should subscribe to some type of policies as we find in Civil Service positions. One advances just so many notches with regard to salary and then he can go to a higher bracket ONLY if *additional responsibilities* are added to his work. If an individual does the SAME thing from one year to the next, WHY should he advance in salary remuneration? If a student does the same type of thinking from one test to another, he generally receives the same grade. WHY CAN'T TEACHING PERSONNEL BE PUT IN THE SAME CATEGORY AS THE STUDENT? The Boy Scouts of America have their merit badges and they mean a great deal in molding the youth of the future; college personnel have passed the MOLDING STAGE, why continue the merit badges?

21. THE EDUCATIONAL LEADERSHIP IN HIGHER EDUCATION IS ADEQUATE TODAY.

The educational leadership in higher education today is inadequate. Why? For the simple reason that few, if any, college presidents have had any experience or training in Educational Administration which IS required of all high school principals. A mere jaunt through the country visiting various colleges and universities, one will find the president's formal education and training in theology, history, English, foreign languages, science, law, military discipline, etc., but few candidates with any training in Educational Administration. One would expect the head of a medical school to have at least the M.D.; the head of a plumber's union should have had some training in plumbing, but in higher education, such analogy does not seem to apply. Actually, all administrators and faculty members should have to pass certification procedures the same as our elementary- and secondary-public school administrators and teachers. The dismal plight of our public and private schools may be traced *directly* to teacher training institutions which prepare the teaching personnel.

22. PUBLIC EDUCATION IS STEADILY IMPROVING.

Public education in this country is in trouble — serious trouble — particularly in the nation's major cities. In a speech to the

South Carolina Education Association in Columbia, James A. Harris, president of the National Education Association, told it like it is, painting a stark, grim, threatening education picture with these facts: [23]

There are nearly 2 million school-aged children who are not in school. Most of them live in the large cities.

Of the students who are attending classes, more of them will spend some portion of their lives in a correctional institution than those who will attend all the institutions of higher learning.

Take any school day of the year, and you will find 13,000 kids of school-age in correctional institutions and another 100,00 in jail or police-lockups.

Of every 100 students attending school across the nation, 23 drop out, 77 graduate from high school, 43 enter college, 21 receive the B.A., 6 earn an M.A., and 1 earns a Ph.D.

Crime and violence in central city schools are growing at unprecedented rates. In the high schools of some cities literally thousands of students who have no interest in education, roam the corridors, disrupt the classes, constantly look for trouble or foment it.

By acting upon the findings of research, A NEW SYSTEM OF EDUCATION can occur; one which can produce more tax dollars than tax dollars received, one which will bring greater success, purpose, satisfaction, and happiness to each of our citizens.

[1] Kotulak, Ronald, "A.M.A. in age retirement suit," *The Chicago Tribune*, Saturday, May 18, 1974, Section 1, p. 3.

[2] *Today's Education*, December 1971, p. 4.

[3] Leton, Donald A., "An Evaluation of Course Methods in Teaching Child Development," *Journal of Educational Research* 55:118-22; November 1961.

[4] *Review of Educational Research*, October 1965, p. 330.

[5] Aiken, Lewis R., Jr., "The Grading Behavior of a College Faculty," *Educational and Psychological Measurement* 23:319-22, Summer 1963.

6Reprinted with permission of the Industrial Management Society from Vol. 15, No. 10, October 1973 INDUSTRIAL MANAGEMENT.

7Gentry, Castelle and Charles Johnson, *A Practical Management System For Performance-Based Teacher Education*, American Association of Colleges for Teacher Education, February 1974, p. 1.

8Hilgard, Ernest R. *Theories of Learning* (2d ed.; New York: Appleton-Century-Crofts, Inc., 1956), p. 457.

9Bugelski, B. R. *The Psychology of Learning Applied to Teaching* (New York: Bobbs-Merrill Co., Inc., 1964), p. 14.

10Mayer, Martin. *Where, When, and Why: Social Studies in American Schools* (New York: Harper and Row, Publishers, 1963), pp. 131-132.

11Blanchard, B. Everard, "A Schematic Analysis of Extension Course Programs in Institutions of Higher Education," *The New Campus,* Association for Field Services in Teacher Education, Vol. XX, Spring, 1967, p. 54.

12*Ibid.,* p. 55.

13*Developments*, From the Child Development Institute, University of North Carolina, Chapel Hill, Frank Porter Graham Child Development Center, Vol. 1, No. 3, Spring, 1974, p. 1.

14*The Chronicle of Higher Education*, Vol. VIII, No. 18, February 4, 1974, p. 1.

15Blanchard, B. Everard, "Our Maladjusted Entrance Requirements," *Improving College and University Teaching*, Vol. XX, No. 3, Summer 1972, p. 123.

16Wallace, Andrew, "College recruiting: personnel's vast wasteland," *The Personnel Administrator*, March-April 1972, p. 22

17Wallace, Andrew. *To Hell on a Mortar Board*. Trend Publications, Inc., P.O. Box 2350, Tampa, Florida 33601, 1972, p. 6.

18Wallace, Andrew C., "Education in Business Administration — Image and Implications," *Collegiate News and Views*, Vol. XXV, No. 4, Summer, 1972, p. 2.

19*Ibid.,* p. 2.

20*Ibid.,* p. 2.

21Heller, H.J., "Gifted children: 'Most neglected minority in education?' "*Chicago Sun-Times*, Sunday, February 10, 1974, p. 88

22*Intellect*, "Evaluation — International Study of Achievement in Science, Reading, and Literature," Vol. 102, No. 2351, October 1973, p. 5.

23Parade's Special, Edited by Lloyd Shearer, "Education — Too Little, Too Late," *The Chicago Sun-Times*, Sunday, June 16, 1974, p. 5.

INDEX OF NAMES

INDEX OF SUBJECTS